FOLLOWING THE SUN AND MOON

FOLLOWING THE SUN AND MOON

Hopi Kachina Tradition

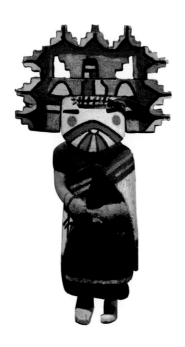

by Alph H. Secakuku

Landscape Photography by Owen Seumptewa

Object Photography by Craig Smith

Northland Publishing
in cooperation with The Heard Museum

Dedicated to the Hopi People.
Our greatest bond is our Hopi religion—
giving us the strength and unity for
time immemorial.

Text type was set in Meridien
Display type was set in Felix Titling
Designed by Lisa MacCollum
Art directed by Trina Stahl
Edited by Stephanie Bucholz
Production supervised by Lisa Brownfield

Manufactured in Hong Kong by Regent Publishing Services

FIRST IMPRESSION
ISBN 0-87358-632-8 (hardcover)
ISBN 0-87358-644-1 (softcover)

Library of Congress Catalog Card Number 95-9163
Cataloging-in-Publication Data
Following the sun and moon : Hopi Kachina tradition / by Alph H. Secakuku ; landscape photography by Owen Seumptewa ; object photography by Craig Smith. — 1st ed.
p. cm.
Includes bibliographical references (p.   ) and index.
ISBN 0-87358-632-8 (hc). — ISBN 0-87358-644-1 (pbk.)
1. Hopi Indians—Rites and ceremonies. 2. Kachinas. 3. Kachina dolls. 4. Hopi mythology.
5. Hopi Indians—Religion. I. Title.
E99.H7S345 1995
299'.74—dc20   95-9163
                                                               CIP

Cover Photo: *The male Wakaskatsina is an animal spirit messenger to the Rain gods*
(see page 41).

0561/1M/8-95 (hc)
0561/9M/8-95 (sc)

CONTENTS

FOREWORD

In 1975 The Heard Museum published a catalogue of the Barry Goldwater collection of Hopi kachina dolls. Arizona's senior statesman had donated 437 kachina dolls to the Heard a decade earlier. With the popular 1975 catalogue no longer in print, the museum has for some time considered how to publish its collection of kachina dolls, including historic pieces from the Fred Harvey Fine Arts Collection.

Following the Sun and Moon combines spectacular photographs of the collection with sensitive commentary by a Hopi author. Many well-researched and informative books have come to print from non-Hopi people. This book contributes the intimate perspective only someone like Alph H. Secakuku (himself a carver) can offer.

An important goal of this publication is to foster understanding and greater respect for the Hopi way of life. The kachina doll has meaning far beyond its appeal as an exotic collectible. Each carving offers unique and powerful insight into the beauty of Hopi culture.

Sadly, the Hopi people have had to contend with overly curious admirers who insist on knowing—or even imitating—all that can be known about their beliefs and practices. True tolerance respects privacy where it is appropriate. The Heard Museum expresses our sincere gratitude to those knowledgeable Hopi individuals who commented on the manuscript. We hope that this publication achieves the difficult but essential balance between freedom of ideas and respect for privacy.

Many thanks to Alph H. Secakuku, who accepted the challenging assignment of authorship. The Heard Museum's director of research, Ann Marshall, coordinated the book's production with enormous skill and diplomacy. Lisa MacCollum, exhibits and graphics coordinator at the museum, deserves applause for the book's design. Photographs, by Craig Smith and Owen Seumptewa, contribute warmth and depth; Mary Dieterich's initial editing brought clarity. Gloria Lomahaftewa and Ramson Lomatewama provided indispensable guidance in selection of carvings, while Delbridge Honanie and Clifford Lomahaftewa greatly assisted with identification of the carvings.

MARTIN SULLIVAN
Director, The Heard Museum

A NOTE FROM THE AUTHOR

Though the word *kachina* is widely used to refer to the spiritual beings and dolls of the Pueblo Indian religions, it is inaccurate in the Hopi language, which has no *ch* sound. *Katsina* is a more accurate translation of the Hopi spoken word and is preferred by those who speak the Hopi language. Also, the glossary of Hopi words is an orthographic representation of the Second Mesa dialect.

The Second Mesa Hopi village Supawlavi is the home of the author, Alph H. Secakuku. This village was settled shortly after the Pueblo Indian Revolt in 1680.

All too often, in the view of many Hopi people, information about Hopi ceremonies is purposely distorted to portray highly dramatized or picturesque versions, ignoring spiritual context and religious significance. Some feel that accounts of this type have created too much public awareness and interest in the Hopi, resulting in intrusion by outsiders and the closure of many Hopi ceremonies to non-Indians. Also, accurate as well as inaccurate published accounts have been misused as public guides to replicate Hopi ceremonies for profit or to observe closed ceremonies, constituting intrusion on the Hopi way of life. This book is meant for educational purposes only, not as a public guide.

Many Hopi people simply feel their way of life has been exploited and misrepresented by the non-Hopi, and are reluctant to provide in-depth information about their religion with visitors (tourists) and even non-Hopi friends. Perhaps the worst fear is that knowledge shared either as a matter of courtesy or as privileged information might later turn up in written accounts—especially if presented inaccurately and attributed by name. Hopi people are generally apprehensive of the ridicule they may receive in the community for providing information to non-Hopi people about their culture. The people who shared information with me for this book requested their names not be mentioned because they know—too well—no published material will ever meet the general approval of the Hopi people. It is not a cultural value to convert people to the Hopi ways.

No doubt there will be Hopi people who will object to my publication of this book, who will construe it as an intrusion into their religious privacy. They believe that the Hopi religion is a private matter and that there is already too much information on Hopi in the mass media. They believe that the Hopi way of life has been exploited and misrepresented by the non-Hopi and that some information is purposely distorted to reflect the opinion of the writer, and/or is inaccurate. They believe that no person, especially a Hopi, should make money from any part of the Hopi culture by writing magazine articles or books, sketching, recording, photographing, or producing videotapes or movies depicting the Hopi way of life. Advocates of the recent copyright issue believe that information about the Hopi constitutes their intellectual property and should be protected.

While I understand some of the reasons for these beliefs, I do not completely agree with them. My life objective is to preserve the beauty and the value of our belief system rather than watch it die out. There are many people who, like myself, have been greatly influenced by the twentieth century and acculturated into the dominant society, but still strive to perpetuate our belief system through practice. Participation, however, is carried out at our convenience either because much of the religious system has been discontinued at the village where we live, or because we are employed full-time. There are some younger Hopis who do not currently have the benefit of the full religious experience or memory of the past as a resource. Our culture is very much alive, but I believe we need to preserve our cultural information and, at the same time, counteract the history of exploitation and misrepresentation.

One way to do this is through the educational process. The world has shrunk to a point where we cannot be strangers any longer. Like it or not, we are no longer isolated and must change our views and lifestyles as the world changes. I believe we must participate in and contribute to world technology. Our way of life can survive only if we recognize and interact with, not ignore, modern development. "Interact with the world and take from it what is valuable—let go of what is not life beneficial" is one Hopi philosophy. My objective is to provide invaluable information about the Hopi, for the Hopi, based on my own knowledge and experience.

I want to thank the people who assisted me in my efforts to explain and show the "why," and not the "how," of the greatness and endurance of the Hopi life ways. *Kwakha.*

PREFACE

The complex cycle of interrelated responsibilities and concepts that is the Hopi religious system is all the more complicated because each of the twelve Hopi villages possesses the autonomy to carry out Hopi religious practices independently. The timing of ceremonies, the precise rituals involved, even the philosophical responses to the underlying concepts may vary among the Hopi villages. Also, because the Hopi religion is so old and complex, and has no written tribal language, the philosophical responses to the underlying concepts of the katsina dolls surely vary among the Hopi people themselves. Nevertheless, throughout the land of the Hopi, the religious mission is the same: to promote and achieve a "unity" of everything in the universe.

Change is an inherent part of human culture, and the forces of the twentieth century cannot be denied. There are several publications that present "modern" interpretations of the katsina dolls, their meanings, practices, and uses. There also exist many accounts, mostly by non-Hopi people, that reflect what they have researched or interpreted or been told by various Hopi people. In spite of the language barrier and the multifaceted nature of Hopi culture, with its variations from village to village (not to mention the secrecy of much of the Hopi ceremonial cycle, even among the Hopi), some of these publications provide excellent reference material and sources of understanding. They are listed in the "Further Reading" section.

Indeed, the Hopi religion is so old and complex that it is impossible for any one Hopi, or even a traditional political faction or group within Hopi, to know it in its entirety. Beware of any one person professing to be the traditional spokesman for Hopi or even the "traditional" Hopi. No one person could possibly speak for the Hopi. Some who profess to do so, in fact, do not practice the beliefs of the Hopi religion nor participate in its priesthoods. The text herein is only one man's interpretation, and is not meant to represent the Hopi view: Hopi individuals are taught cultural values and concepts at an early age by their clan relations and respective societal godfathers. This book is a record of my own experiences, based on the voices from past generations, and I firmly believe that in these voices lies the primary value of my experience.

My objective in this publication is to present the Hopi and their ceremonial calendar from a Hopi's point of view—to provide a brief, general description of each important ceremony in the Hopi religious cycle, focusing on the katsina tradition, which is the main subject of this publication. These accounts are based on my own experiences and knowledge of the ceremonies as practiced on Second Mesa, one of the three high mesas of the Hopi Reservation in northeastern Arizona. I have left out those parts of the Hopi ceremonies that are too sacred to be discussed. My hope is that non-Hopi people will gain from these accounts a deeper understanding and respect for the Hopi way. I hope too that Hopi readers, especially the young, will be stimulated to search for a deeper understanding and appreciation of their own religious practices.

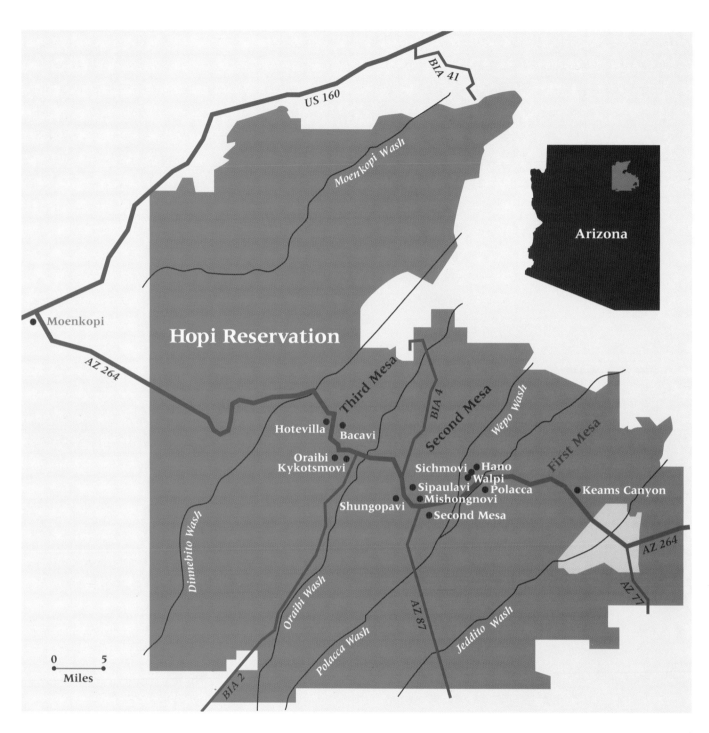

Map of Hopiland showing the Hopi villages. Note that spellings of village names reflect road signs and standard maps, not Second Mesa dialect.

INTRODUCTION

The Hopi culture is very difficult to define in a precise manner. Our social and political structures are divided into numerous powerful kinship groups. This kinship or extended family system is called the Hopi Clans. Clan membership is traced through the mother. Clan members are the guardians of their respective ritual knowledge and share clan contributions and duties in the overall Hopi religious practices.

As a cultural entity, the Hopi share many values, attitudes and a way of life that others do not share. For example, based on our religious beliefs, we all share inner feelings about our caretaker responsibilities for the land and the purposes for which we are on it. Because of our historical experiences, and, more importantly, because of our values, we act and make judgments in ways that sometimes an "outsider" cannot understand. The things shared by the Hopi are race, religion, language, traditions, historical experiences, and values.

The Hopi people have lived on the three high mesas of northern Arizona for time immemorial. Of ninety-five hundred tribal members today, about sixty-five hundred live in twelve villages on the Hopi Reservation: Walpi, Sitsomóvi, and Hano on First Mesa; Musangnuvi, Supawlavi, and Songoopavi on Second Mesa; Orayvi, Kiqötsmovi, Hotvela, and Paaqavi on Third Mesa; and, thirty-five miles west of Hotvela, the villages of Upper and Lower Mungapi.

Generally, these villages are independent, exercising traditional self-government and carrying out their own religious cycles. For socioeconomic purposes, most Hopis are affiliated with one village or another, but virtually all Hopi persons claim "home" to be the village in which their mothers were born, since one's clan and extended family derive from the maternal lineage.

For the purpose of dealing with the influences of the twentieth century and the outside world generally, a Hopi Tribal Council was established on December 19, 1936, representing the union of self-governing villages. This political organization operates under a constitution and bylaws delegated to it by the general tribal membership. It maintains a government-to-government relationship with state and county agencies, as well as with the federal government, which acts as a legal trustee for the Hopi Tribe.

The Hopi lands are relatively barren and very dry, having an annual rainfall of five to seven inches. Even so, the Hopi are grateful to the supreme deity, *Maasawu* (Earth god), for entrusting the land to the Hopi soon after their arrival on what is known to the Hopi as the Fourth World. At that time the Hopi leaders and wisemen made sacred vows to Maasawu, who assigned them responsibility as care-takers of the Fourth World or Mother Earth—the land the Hopi call *Tuuwaqatsi* (earth), the Hopi *tutskwa* (land).

To keep their promise of entrusting the Hopi with responsibility as caretakers of Mother Earth, and to sustain the wholeness of all things in great balance, the supreme deity and his priests guided the Hopi in the development of a complex and multifaceted religion based on the philosophy that all things, living or not, are melded into a great wholeness. The Hopi Clan system, their unique relationship with the land and animals, their prayers for rain and snow for the sustenance of life—all this is part of the Hopi religion. To maintain the harmony of the world, and to achieve bountiful harvests and the replenishment of sacred springs, the Hopi secure meditative relation-ships with supernatural beings through positive concepts and processes. Some parts of the sacred processes are secret, performed only by high priesthood leaders.

The Hopi believe their greatest bond is their religion. It has given them the strength to resist external forces and has kept them united for centuries. It has also helped to maintain the *Hopituy* (uniquely Hopi) rapport with their land, which they proudly refer to as *tuuwanasavi*—the spiritual center of the earth. Tuuwanasavi is very special to the Hopi *sinom* (people) because it was established and developed during their migration of the Tuuwaqatsi.

OVERVIEW

HOPI RELIGIOUS CEREMONIES

The day for beginning a ceremony is determined by the sunrise or sunset, depending on the time of year, and this beginning point is confirmed by such lunar observations as the first day or night of the new moon.

A *kikmongwi* (village chief) and the leaders of the priesthood societies gather for a special blessing ceremony and perform ritual prayers and meditation that, in the fullest sense, are from the heart. This special blessing ceremony constitutes the formal declaration of the coming ceremony. At sunrise, the village crier makes a public announcement of the ceremony.

All the days of the ceremony are important, as they are spent performing secret rituals in the *kiva*. In all ceremonies, the participants must be in a deep spiritual mode and attain a harmonious unity that manifests the wholeness of life and all things, to insure that prayers for life-sustaining moisture are fulfilled. A ceremonial dance is then performed for the public, giving the people an opportunity to meditate and offer prayers.

Each ceremony is different. Some may be led by priesthood leaders of a specific clan and others are led by priesthood leaders ordained with specific ceremonial duties. Some are highly sacred, while others, such as the social dances, are quasi-religious entertainment. Some, like the wedding ceremony, are performed for special purposes. Whatever the purpose, *all* Hopi ceremonies are highly spiritual in content, and should be viewed, conducted, and respected as such.

HOPI KATSINAM

The *katsinam* are the benevolent spirit beings who live among the Hopi for about a six-month period each year. They first arrive during *Soyalwimi* in December and begin to appear in greater number during the *Powamuya* ceremonial season (in February), and return to their spirit world after the *Niman* ceremony (in July). The Powamuya dramatizes the final stages of world creation, and calls upon the katsina spirit beings to invoke substantial growth and maturity for all mankind. The katsina spirits are, therefore, the very important, meaningful, and beneficial counterpart in a relationship invaluable to the Hopi religious beliefs. Accordingly, we do not perceive the

These mesas, located on Hopiland some distance from the villages, are known as the Katsina Points. The San Francisco Peaks can be seen in the background.

katsina dolls simply as carved figurines or brightly decorated objects. They have important meaning to us, the Hopi people: We believe they are personifications of the katsina spirits, originally created by the katsinam in their physical embodiment. They are presented to females by the spirits as personalized gifts to award virtuous behavior and to publicly recognize special persons, such as brides, who are presented at the Niman ceremony.

The katsina dolls first appear in the ceremonial calendar in February during Powamuya, the bean dance season. At sunrise on the day of the dance, the *Qöqöqlom* and/or other katsinam appear bearing colorful, invaluable gifts of katsina dolls, decorative plaques, dancing wands, lightning sticks, rattles, moccasins, and many other traditional gifts for their friends, the village people. These valued gifts are mainly to award the appropriate behavior of children. The morning ritual also includes a gift for the matriarch of each house: a bundle of bean sprouts ritually manifested by the katsinam, representing the nourishing crops of the coming season. It is an important time for reunion of the family and for partaking of the bean sprouts and other traditional sacred foods to prolong the blessings everyone has received.

As the ceremonial calendar moves to the *Angk'wa* (katsina night dances) and on to the katsina day dances, emphasis is on gifts of food such as baked sweet corn, other vegetables, and fruits, all samples of food that will be harvested in abundance.

The coming of the Niman ceremony also involves all sorts of invaluable gifts, including the katsina dolls. The katsinam have been on earth in their physical form since the winter solstice season, and, in general, "life" has now blossomed because of the powerful blessings of the supernatural beings' involvement in the cycles of ceremonial rituals. It is now midsummer, and time for the katsinam to return home to their spirit world. Also, it is a time for the most intense prayer and meditation in the Hopi village.

In the Niman ceremony the handsome *Nimankatsinam*, also known as the *Hemiskatsinam*, accompanied by their pretty katsina maidens, bring such traditional gifts as stalks of corn, melons, katsina dolls, and bows and arrows, and dance and provide special blessings throughout the day. (In some villages, other katsinam now perform the Niman ceremony.) Their gifts represent bounty of harvest, and great virtues of life for all mankind. All kinds of katsina dolls are presented to the females representing their different stages and ages. For example, a newborn receiving her first doll will be presented with a simple flat doll, while one who has been initiated into the katsina beliefs that year will receive an elaborately created doll. Finally, to symbolize special blessings for ideal motherhood, each bride of that year will receive a real, lifelike katsina doll. This is a special day for a bride as she is presented by her mother-in-law to the spirits, whom she will join in life after death, and she will be buried—as she is presented—in her wedding robe. The day after the Nimankatsina dance, the katsinam return home to their spirit world. The eagles that are collected in May and adopted into families must also be sent home, bearing prayers and their observations of events in the Hopi world. When the Niman ceremony is completed, the spectacular katsina season comes to a peaceful end, and the people solemnly return to their homes to prepare for the next ceremonies and to carry out their domestic activities.

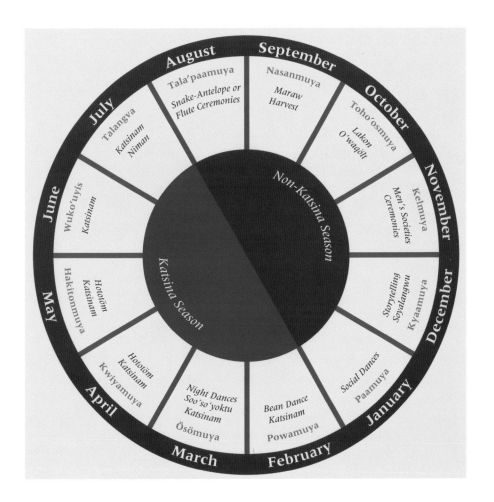

FOURTH WORLD CREATION

KELMUYA

Each year, the Hopi religious calendar is formalized and decreed in November during the *Kelmuya* season. ("Muya" comes from *Muuyawu*, which means "moon.") The ceremonial participants are restricted to those who have completed the "manhood" initiation, during which they proudly commemorate and celebrate the wholeness of the creation of the Fourth World, which is the world we live in today.

After the public announcement of the ceremony, the society members not only prepare for the ceremony, but purify their minds and spirit to achieve humility and peace of mind. In their respective kiva, they perform religious rituals so sacred and secret that no one talks about them, for these ceremonies are only for Hopi priests who have completed their religious instructions.

To complete the ceremony, a public dance is performed in which the people can offer heartfelt prayers in silence to the supernatural beings. The dance, which is not only colorful but spiritually powerful, starts at one kiva and moves through the narrow village streets into the plaza, and back to the starting point kiva. The singing is loud and deep and echoes the drumbeats, which are prayers for long and pleasant life for all mankind, moisture in the form of snow and rain, and a bountiful harvest of nourishing crops.

The power and beauty of the dance are in its guidance by the energies of the supreme deity and his priests, the supernatural beings. Since it is the first great ceremony of the ceremonial cycle, the fire of life is lit, the emergence from the underworld proudly commemorated, germination of life on earth supplicated, and the eternal path of life for all mankind proudly set.

Ahöla is a priest katsina of high order. He is commonly referred to as the Ahölwutaqa, meaning that he is an elderly, wise chief. He is one of the winter solstice katsinam who appear at Powamuya to open the katsina season. Seeds of various plants and crops, which the accompanying katsina maiden brings for each household, are ritually consecrated by the supernatural beings in a kiva. As a messenger, Ahölwutaqa carries to the supernatural beings prayers for a long and healthful life, and peace in the world.

LEFT: *Ahölatmana'at is a katsinmana (katsina maiden) who accompanies the Ahöla as he blesses the village houses. She carries in a basket new seeds that have been ritually consecrated for the completeness of life. At each home, the matriarch takes a handful and carefully puts it in a family seed pot. The seeds are blessed by the katsinam and later planted. During the Niman ceremony, several maidens usually accompany the Hemiskatsinam.*

OPPOSITE: *Left to right: 1) Ewtoto is a katsina spiritual father, an important member of the katsina priesthood order. He appears several times during the Powamuya season, and again during Niman ceremony (Home Dance) in July. He assumes leadership of all the katsina blessing ceremonies because he knows all the ceremonial rituals. 2) Áholi appears during the Powamuya season. During the ceremony he accompanies the Ewtoto, complementing him in performing ceremonial rituals. Like the Ewtoto, he has been spiritually empowered to assist in carrying out the most sacred ceremonial rituals for the benefit of all mankind.*

NEW LIFE FOR THE WORLD

KYAAMUYA

This period, sometime during December, is a time of reverence and respect for the spirit beings (*Kyaa* connotes reverence for the period). It is a time for storytelling and the performance of the *Soyal* ceremony.

STORYTELLING

At this time wise elders, those who know the scope of history, tell stories of the past. When telling adult stories of real events, the storyteller uses the formal language of Hopi; stories for children are usually in the simpler form of parables and the childhood Hopi language, implying a moral lesson. Both emphasize the importance of the past as a moral guide, and the maintenance of the high standards of Hopi life.

SOYALANGWU (PERIOD OF THE SOYAL CEREMONY)

Soyalwimi is performed at the arrival of *Kyaamuya* (the winter solstice season), the sunrise and lunar observations again setting the time for the ceremony. It accepts, confirms and implements the life plan for the year, which has been manifested by the *Wuutsimwimi* (sacred ceremony of one of the sacred religious orders for men). The katsinam appear for the first time during this period.

The *Sivuktsinavitu*, a pair representing the energy of fertility for mankind, are the katsina spirits who physically appear and journey through the village, making copulatory gestures to women to promote the procreation of life. They also carry prayers to the supreme deity and his supernatural associates for healthy life in a healthy environment, and for peace in the world.

No colorful public dance is performed during Soyalwimi. Instead, its religious significance derives throughout from rituals in the kiva, where it includes reverent silence, fasting for purification and humility, and the eating of sacred Hopi foods to achieve prolonged spiritual concentration and dedication.

Upon completion of the ceremony, when the people are offering their silent prayers, *Paamuya* (winter social dances) are being laid out.

Lenangkatsina is a Soyalkatsina, appearing during winter solstice season. Since he is a leader, he performs ceremonial rituals marking the beginning of the katsina season. The Lenangmana supports him in the germination rituals of seeds of life.

*Lenangmana is a female being who
ritually supports the germination of the
seeds of life. She is the katsina maiden to
the Lenangkatsina.*

ABOVE: *Qaletaqa is a Warrior katsina possessing supernatural powers to protect and insure that nothing interrupts the ceremonial rituals. He appears during the Soyal ceremony, safeguarding during the execution of ceremonial rituals. He whirls his bullroarer to bring sounds of thunder and rain.*

OPPOSITE: *Awhalaynikatsina appears during Soyalwimi (winter solstice ceremony), and journeys through the village accompanied by two katsina maidens. The maidens carry corn that has been consecrated in the kiva, and which they deliver to each household. Left to right: 1) Awhalayni appears in the year the Flute ceremony is going to be held in the ceremonial cycle. 2) Awhalayni also appears when the Snake-Antelope ceremony is scheduled for the summer. He sings a special song that is a prayer in itself.*

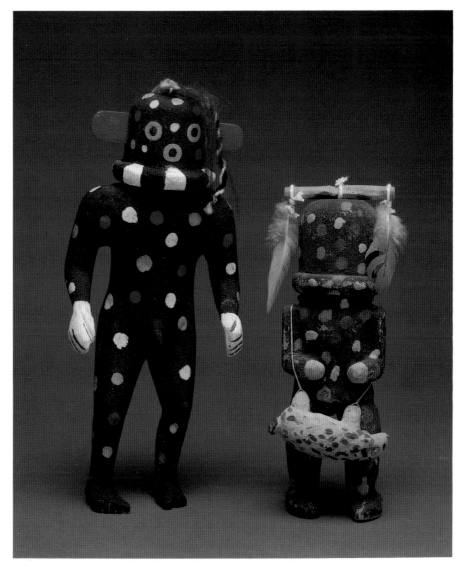

ABOVE: *Left to right: 1) Kokosorhoya appears during the Powamuya ceremony (Bean Dance) in February, accompanying the Ahöla and his katsina maiden as they all play their role in consecration of seeds of life. The Kokosors spirit causes the seeds to sprout or develop to enhance crop growth. He possesses the powers of germination, a healthy beginning for plant life. Kokosorhoya is a young katsina who is innocent and pure of heart, thus possessing the greatest spiritual powers. 2) Sola'wutsi is a Zuni Fire God. He is one of many katsinam who migrated from Zuni, and appears for the Hopi during Angk'wa (March katsina night dances) when the spirits of Zuni Salako visit the Hopi. He carries a torch signifying his responsibility as caretaker of one of the important physical elements of the universe: fire. He brings wild game for the village, choosing a matriarch of a clan, who ritually adopts him into her extended clan family. He is not related to the Kokosorhoya.*

WINTER SOCIAL DANCES

PAAMUYA

Paamuya, "moisture moon," comes in January. It is marked by "social" dances held at night in the kiva or homes, or in the plaza by day. The most common of these dances are versions of the Buffalo Dance, the Hopi versions, or other Pueblo buffalo dances in which other animals are represented as well. Typically, the human participants are two unmarried women, beautifully dressed in traditional ceremonial clothing and traditional hairstyles, and their male partners, costumed and impersonating buffalo.

All social dances are carefully planned, choreographed, and rehearsed in the days before the performances. The dances depicting the animals that roam in the wild wooded mountains now covered by snow represent prayers for winter snow on Hopi fields, and for successful hunting. The songs and movements of these dances symbolically invoke the sanction of the game animals for the sacrifice they will make to supply the Hopi with nourishment.

Paamuya, then, is festive and joyous social activity. Remembering these times during the short days and long nights of winter inspires among the Hopi a deeper reverence for this world. This is a non-katsina ceremony.

OPPOSITE: *Walpi is one of the Hopi villages on First Mesa. Walpi has been officially declared a historic site by the federal government.*

PURIFICATION OF LIFE

POWAMUYA

The Powamuya is perhaps the most complex of all Hopi ceremonies. It implores the katsinam to appear among the Hopi so life for all mankind can have substantial growth and maturity. Usually it begins in February with the appearance of *Ahöla* (a katsina priest of high order) at sunrise. The Ahöla blesses all the houses in the village, and symbolically "opens" the ceremonial chambers for the divine visitations of the katsinam.

All the males initiated into the katsina beliefs go to their kiva where specific rituals are performed in preparation for *totokya* (in this case, the dance day). The Whipper katsinam (powerful spirit beings) congregate at night, and make their way throughout the village. These benevolent visits also serve to evaluate whether or not life standards maintained by the village have been acceptable and warrant special blessings.

Children ten to fifteen years of age are initiated into the katsina beliefs during this ceremony, and they will continue to receive guidance toward their spiritual growth in the katsina beliefs.

The day of the dance, the Qöqöqlom and/or other katsinam appear at sunrise with colorful gifts for their friends, the village people. They give the matriarch of each house a small bundle of bean sprouts—a miraculously manifest sample of the nourishing crops that are the promise of the coming season.

Female children, who are especially honored among the Hopi, receive traditionally created katsina dolls, dancing wands for social dances, decorative plaques, traditional shoes, and other traditional gifts. Male children receive such gifts as colorful lightning sticks, rattles, and moccasins. As valued gifts, they tell a child that he or she has behaved in accordance with standards approved by the friendly katsina spirits.

At Powamuya, the children receive invaluable gifts tied to the bundle of bean sprouts given by the katsinam.

Angwusnasomtaqa is a katsina Mother. She portrays many roles and performs many functions. In this instance, she participates in the initiation blessings of the young children (ages ten to fifteen years) into the katsina beliefs and culture. She guides the Whipper katsinam, who are considered to be her children. She displays an aggressive temperament and is furiously active, insuring that she receives attention in order to deliver to the initiates her message of the importance and significance of the katsina culture. The doll on the left is a newer version of the more traditional doll on the right.

Tungwivkatsinam are the Mongkatsinam, chief katsinam having leadership duties and responsibilities. They are members of the Whipper family and appear during Powamuya ceremony.

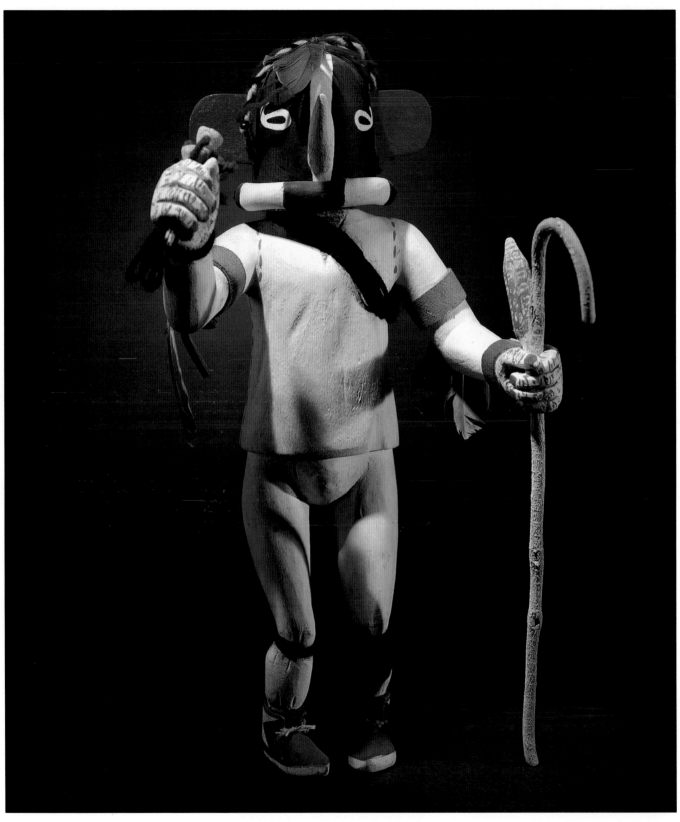

Kokopölö is a katsina with a humpback. He is not a Flute player, though he has been mistakenly referred to as such. He has several functions and appears during Angk'wa, either with a group of Kokopölö katsinam or singly with the mixed katsina group. He is a fertility spirit, one who is capable of sustaining abundant life growth—plant and human.

Left to right: 1 & 3) Powamuykatsinam appear on the day of the Powamuya ceremony. They are the first to set the schedule for Angk'wa. Only persons who are initiated into the katsina societal rites are allowed to witness the performance. Finely ground white cornmeal is worn on the faces. 2) Lenangkatsinam, who also appear during the Powamuya ceremony, are a separate group from the Powamuykatsinam. Their ceremonial dress is different and their faces are sakwa (blue). They also are accompanied by maidens.

TOP: *Angwusnasomtaqa is one of the Mothers of the katsinam; as such, she responds to ceremonial actions and the calling of her katsina children for various purposes. She leads the performance and the special functions, such as the katsina initiation of Hopi children. She is well versed in moral principles and the virtues of life, appearing with stately elegance and dignity.*

BOTTOM: *Left to right: 1) Kwikwilyaqa is a Clown katsina who mimics actions of people or other katsinam. He contributes much humor to the society. 2) Hiilili is a Whipper katsina whose family appears during the Powamuya ceremony and Angk'wa. 3) Sikyaqöqlo is the artist, practicing the art of agrarian culture and producing the colorful gifts that he brings for children at the Powamuya ceremony. 4) Sootukwnang is a Star katsina whose name connotes master or manager of the universe. He appears during the Angk'wa, usually with the mixed katsina group. He carries a lightning bolt and a bull-roarer to make thundering sounds during his visit.*

Left to right: 1) Mastopkatsina is a member of the Soyalkatsinam. He appears only on Third Mesa, a counterpart of Second Mesa's Sivuktsina. These Soyalkatsinam come in pairs, representing the energy of fertility for mankind. They make copulatory gestures to women to promote the procreation of life. 2) Áholi is a Soyalkatsina on Third Mesa. He performs sacred rituals during Soyal ceremony, complementing the Ewtoto. 3) Tuvatsqöqlo appears during Powamuya ceremony, bringing gifts of bean sprouts and colorful gifts for the children. The Qöqlo family come in various colors representing the six directions (north, west, south, east, universe, and the underworld). The Black Qöqlo talk "backwards"—the nature of their speech has the opposite meaning. If they say "It's not a good day," they actually mean that it is a beautiful and pleasant day.

TOP: *Left to right: 1) Ma'lokatsina is an old traditional katsina belonging to the early period of katsina development among the Hopi. He performs a dance that portrays a prayer for rain. 2) Sikyaqöqlo appears at the Powamuya ceremony, performing several functions. He portrays an image of being very artistic, the one responsible for producing and distributing crops and colorful gifts for the children. In addition, he practices the art of storytelling. Sikyaqöqlo may appear with the mixed katsina group during Angk'wa. 3) Hahay'iwuuti is a katsina Mother who has several ceremonial functions. She responds to different situations or ceremonial events, such as Hopi Salako, Powamuya, and Angk'wa, as either a leader or a guide. She is a very energetic, sprightful, talkative being. She always carries her ceremonial water jug, the kuy'wiki (water that has been blessed).*

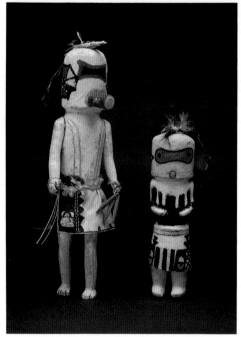

BOTTOM: *Sipiknitaqa is a Whipper katsina guard who performs security functions during the katsina rituals in Angk'wa, insuring safety for the katsinam. He appears either with a group of Sipiknikatsinam or singly with other katsinam, such as the Hopi version of Zuni Salako or the Whipper katsinam during Powamuya ceremony. Sipiknikatsinam portray honorable characters and serve as excellent protectors of katsinam. They maintain order among the people and the katsina Clowns such as the Koyemsimu, or Mudheads (a non-Hopi term derived from the use of mud on the masks of these katsinam). Sipiknikatsinam appear in different colors, representing different directions. Their dancing is spirited, demanding a lot of energy.*

Ewizro is a Warrior katsina, one who punishes and maintains order. He appears during the Powamuya ceremony and the summer katsina day dances. He declares war on the human clowns for their blatant, mischievous and unacceptable behavior of poking fun at the people and the Pivtukam (katsina Clowns).

Wupamokatsina is a guard who makes his appearance during the Powamuya, supervising the Whipper katsinam and insuring reverence and respect for the katsinam. He is usually harassed by the Koyemsihoyam (young Mudheads), who convey their mischievousness by pulling on the ceremonial dress of the Wupamokatsina. The Wupamokatsina, usually treated with great dignity, whips the Koyemsihoyam to correct their behavior. The doll on the right is an older, more traditional doll than the two on the left.

ABOVE: *Left to right: 1) Tsanayo appears during Powamuya ceremony. He is a Mongkat-sina, appearing only to perform ceremonial rituals. He has a Snake decoration on his face. 2) Tsitoto is a Flower katsina, bringing the great beauty of different flowers and plant life for pleasantness on earth. This katsina appears during Powamuya ceremony and Angk'wa. He sings a special song that is a prayer in itself. 3) Kwewu is a Wolf katsina appearing with other animal katsinam, serving as a guard or a herder. He dances in line with the katsinam, and at certain phases within songs will come out to the side and dance, insuring that nothing is both-ering the dancers. He is very colorful, as well as forceful in appearance. He appears during Angk'wa and the summer katsina day dances. All the animal dances are prayers for rain and an increase of game animals. 4) Hiilili is a Whipper katsina, a guard or security figure. Dressed in the Snake dancer's costume, he is a very spirited dancer, appearing during Powamuya, Angk'wa, and the summer katsina day dances. 5) Hee'e'e is a Warrior katsina maiden or female leader. She is a mana (unmarried maiden). As such her hair is worn in the style of unmarried maidens: on one side in a butterfly whorl. She only appears during Powamuya ceremony to lead the family of Whipper katsinam into the village.*

OPPOSITE: *Muyingwa is a Germination god possessing the great knowledge and duties related to agriculture. He ritually insures that the processes for plant life will properly develop and the plants sprout for eventual life sustenance. He is one of the Mongkatsinam and appears singly with the mixed katsina group.*

ABOVE: *Aalosaka is a supreme being, a deity of the Two-Horn society. He is revered by the society members as supremely whole-some and spiritually powerful. He is one of the Mongkatsinam, appearing singly with the mixed katsina group.*

OPPOSITE: *Motsinkatsinam get their name from their disheveled hair. Their function and duty are to carry out public order, such as policing public works projects, and to insure that all village men are present to render assistance. They are mean spirits and not afraid to use the whips they carry. They also appear during the Powamuya ceremony and the summer katsina day dances to punish the human clowns for their mischievous actions.*

RIGHT: *Kwikwilyaqa is a Clown katsina who gets his name from the stripes on his nose. He has many different personalities, arising from his ability to mock the personalities and actions of people and katsinam. His purpose is to bring about happiness through humor. People laugh at the misfortunes of those whom he selects to mimic. He appears during the Powamuya ceremony and during the summer katsina day dances. He comes to the human clowns for the purpose of mocking their mischievous behavior, bringing outbursts of laughter from the spectators.*

Left to right: 1 & 4) Hiililikatsinam are from the Whipper family, appearing during Powamuya ceremony. They also perform in group dances during Angk'wa with the Koyemsimu singing to them. The Hiilili on the left (1) is wearing a Snake Dancer's costume. 2 & 3) Haaniiyakatsinam are from the Ogre family, appearing during Powamuya ceremony and Angk'wa. They appear in different body colors. Both of these Haaniiyakatsinam are wearing Snake Dancers' costumes.

TOP: *Left to right: 1) Sootukwnang is a Star katsina who manages the movement of the universe. He appears during Angk'wa and during the summer katsina day dances, usually with the mixed katsina group. 2) Hiilili is a Whipper katsina who appears during Powamuya ceremony, Angk'wa, and the summer katsina day dances. He is very spirited and dances at a fast pace.*

BOTTOM: *Left to right: 1) So'yokwuuti is an older sister in the Ogre family. She has an aggressive, forceful personality and is mean in temperament, always threatening the children's lives. She carries a large burden basket on her back and a long hook for capturing unwary children, whom she threatens to eat because they have been naughty. A family of Ogres appears in February. 2) So'yoktaqa, husband of So'yokwuuti, appears with the Ogre family as a demanding, aggressive personality. He talks in a deep, drawn-out speech when the food that is offered is not to his satisfaction. 3) Tossonkoyemsi is the taster, sampling the kind and quality of the toosi (finely ground sweet cornmeal) to insure that it is placed in the right container. He also helps deliver the food collected to be delivered to the sponsoring kiva. He is not an Ogre, but a relative of the family.*

The purification period continues with the coming of the *Soo'so'yoktu* (the mean Ogre katsina spirits). The coming of the Sosoyoktu to the village is meditated upon and spiritually prepared for in the last stages of Powamuya.

The ceremony begins with the sudden appearance of *So'yokwuuti* (sister of the Ogre family) in the gloom of a winter evening in February. She stops at each home in the village, demanding that female members of the household (usually the young ones) prepare certain sacred foods, which are not only time-consuming to prepare but mastered only by many years of instruction and cooking experience. At the same time, the So'yokwuuti demands that males (especially the young boys), hunt large game animals, which is a difficult task since such hunting requires a great deal of hunting experience and, furthermore, large game animals are not available.

But the So'yokwuuti wants both game and sacred food in great quantities. Only if they are provided will individual life be spared to enjoy the blessings manifested by the completed ceremonies. Within about a week, the Sosoyoktu appear from the *So'yok'ki* (spiritual home of the Ogres) and proceed to each house, insisting on the food. The *Soo'so'yokt* (another word for Ogre family) fill the village with eerie and terrifying hoots and snarls. The peacefulness of the village is shattered. The Ogres say that if the food demanded is not forthcoming, they will take the children and eat them instead. The children wail and cry in terror. Everybody looks into themselves to see what they may have done wrong during the year to deserve this terrifying disruption.

At each house and kiva, everyone (including kiva members) is loudly and publicly ridiculed, harshly disciplined for not living up to the high standards of life. Especially important is the maintenance of the spiritual life crucial for the continuing existence of one's "Hopiness." Once the ridicules and punishments are over, everyone is given a special blessing: a social dance is held as a healing process. The Ogre family is forcibly removed from the village as an antidote for their ridicule and punishments.

Meanwhile, during these festive moments in the village, kiva members are meditating—planning the *Angk'wa*, the night dances of the katsinam.

Nata'aska is a Bigmouth Ogre, an Uncle of the Ogre family. These katsinam appear in pairs, standing in the back of the group, snarling and dragging their saws on the ground, impatiently waiting to be fed by the Koyemsi (a Mudhead). The Nata'aska dance and sing a message to the children that they will eat them and chew their bones, and no one will ever see them again.

ABOVE: *Wiharu is another Ogre, and also an Uncle of the Ogre family. His desire is for fat, greasy foods, which his name connotes. He seeks children who are obese, whose flesh is rich and tasty. His mouth is not as big as that of the Nata'aska.*

RIGHT: *Nata'aska is very impatient and keeps up a steady pace stomping, moving back and forth, singing a song that has a message for naughty children. He will not hesitate to eat the mischievous children.*

Left to right: 1) Hehey'akatsina is not an Ogre, but a relative of the Ogre family. He appears
with the Soo'so'yoktuy during their collection of food. 2) Qötsawihazru is an Uncle of the Ogre
family, a White Ogre. He is a little more patient than the Black Ogres. He is not an active Ogre,
but is still fearsome.

KATSINA NIGHT DANCES

ÖSÖMUYA

During the *Ösömuya*, a season encompassing the month of March, a series of katsina night dances take place in each of the villages. From now until July the katsina rituals and beliefs will be manifested in the lives of the Hopi. The katsinam are ever-watchful spirit beings, the invisible forces of life and messengers who listen for humble prayers and meditations. The immediate goal of the night dances is to create a pleasant atmosphere for all life forms, encourage their growth, and bring all-important rain for their fruitfulness.

ANGK'WA (KATSINA DANCE SERIES OF THE ÖSÖMUYA)

Well after darkness falls on the day designated for the beginning of the Angk'wa, the people enter the kiva and wait reverently for the dances to begin. Suddenly, in the stillness of the night, one can hear faint noises associated with the coming of the katsinam. Then, mysteriously, they arrive on the kiva roof and announce their physical presences with pleasing, beautiful sounds. One or two will then shake their rattles at the kiva opening, signifying to the kiva chief that they have brought good things for their friends, the Hopi people. Excitedly, the kiva chief invites the katsinam to enter and, in single file, they climb down the ladder from the small opening in the roof of the kiva. Once inside, they look around happily at their friends and give them gifts of food, such as baked sweet corn, fruits, and other produce. These gifts are samples of the crops that will grow in abundance during the summer.

One by one, the katsinam take their places in the center of the kiva. Amid loud sounds and rhythmic movement, they create an impression of many like images repeated over and over in mirrors— a happy atmosphere of color, dance and sound. The middle katsina in the line leads by shaking his rattle. Turtle shells clack and clatter, bells jingle, and with a loud and deep chorus of singing the dance begins like a huge cloudburst of sound and motion, a burst of prayer for all life forms.

Palhikmana is a katsina maiden with several functions. She can appear during Angk'wa as a Poliimana (Butterfly maiden) or as a Corn-Grinding maiden, or she can perform a special dance. The sponsoring kiva members must fast, abstaining from eating salty and fatty foods, and abstaining from contact with the opposite sex. Fasting achieves prolonged spiritual concentration and dedication through self-purification of the mind and spirit. It brings about peace of mind for the ceremony. The Koyemsimu sing in full, deep, and loud voices, beating on a large ceremonial drum while the four Palhikmamant are led by the Lenangtaqa. This is a colorful dance that is a prayer for rain and a bountiful harvest.

In all the village kiva, the same events are taking place at the same time, accompanied by the same music and synchronous dancing, and using the same bright ceremonial dress and dance objects (such as bows and arrows, rattles, and evergreen). All combine to create a great and meditative wholeness. For those present, focused as they are on this powerful and harmonious dance, time disappears. Then, with the shake of a rattle, the dancing, singing, and drumming abruptly cease, and in the peacefulness and quiet the beauty and spiritual uplift of the songs echo in one's mind.

In the same divine and majestic fashion as they entered, the katsinam climb up the ladder; they are on their way to another kiva. Another group of katsinam prepare to enter, to reassert their great influence in the kiva. The dances may go on for hours, even until just before dawn. The following day is set aside for feasting and visiting among the Hopi extended families, and may be interrupted by the appearance of katsinam in the plaza.

After each village kiva has had an opportunity to sponsor a night dance, the Angk'wa is complete and the support for life-growth is manifested. Life in the villages is always full of activity. Preparations now begin to take place for the day katsina dances in the plaza. These katsina dances are held during March, April, May, and June.

KATSINA DAY DANCES

Someone, often a woman, may have been especially impressed by the katsinam during a night dance and decide to sponsor a day katsina dance. After their last kiva dance, she proudly requests that they continue their entertainment and spiritual blessings, either the day after the night dance or at a future date set by her.

The schedule for this dance typically takes into account the stages of plant life and the planting of crops. For example, the woman sponsor (or often two women sponsors) may request the katsinam to perform during the *Wuko'uyis*, the main planting season in early June.

Poliimana is a Butterfly maiden appearing during Angk'wa with her Poliitaqa (Butterfly man). This is a colorful dance, usually performed with four pairs of maidens and tataqtu (male partners) forming the dance group.

Birds of different types are represented among the katsinam. From left to right: 1) Kyaro is a Parrot katsina whose bright colorful feathers are used in various Hopi ceremonies. They dance at a fast pace and appear during Angk'wa or the summer katsina day dances. 2) Kwahu is an Eagle katsina, whose feathers are very important in all the Hopi ceremonies. The Eagle dance is a colorful dance and a prayer for moisture, good crop yield, and plentiful eagle feathers. The sponsoring kiva members must fast, abstaining from eating salty and fatty foods, and contact with the opposite sex, before the dance. The Kwahu appear during Angk'wa. 3) Tootsa is a Hummingbird katsina. He dances at a fast pace. His songs are prayers for moisture, and for the flourishing and blooming of nat'wani (home-grown plants, crops, and harvest). These katsinam appear in March during Angk'wa, and the summer katsina day dances, either as a group or singly with the mixed katsina group. 4) Pawikya is a Duck katsina, whose feathers are used by the Hopi.

Pootawikkatsina is a Coiled Plaque Carrier. This katsina brings, as gifts for the people, brightly decorated plaques to focus their attention on the beauty of the earth and its useful resources. The plaques serve as a reminder that humans are the caretakers of Mother Earth, taking from it only what they need. Hopi coiled plaques, made from the earth's plants, are round like the earth and depict various life forms or spirits on earth. This katsina appears during Angk'wa or the summer katsina day dances.

39

Kwahu is an Eagle katsina who appears very occasionally during Angk'wa. There are usually several forming a dance group, imitating the movements of squawking eagles. The Koyemsimu sing to the group. The colorful dance is performed for moisture and bountiful harvest.

ABOVE: *Wakaskatsina is a Cow katsina. The male Wakaskatsina is an animal spirit messenger to the rain gods. His song is a prayer for plentiful animal life, and symbolic of their self-sacrifice as food supply to sustain life. This is an older doll than the dolls on the left.*

LEFT: *Left to right: 1) The male Wakaskatsina is easily identified by his colorful body paint of red, yellow, and blue. The ceremonial clothing of red belt, embroidered sash, and kilt is always worn by males. 2) The female Wakaskatsina, or Wakaskatsinmana, wears traditional women's clothing of manta, cape of red and black, and wedding shoes. The Wakaskatsinam represent animal spirit messengers to the Rain gods. Their songs and dance movements are prayers for rain, and are symbolic of animals' self-sacrifice in supplying food to sustain life.*

ABOVE: *Tsivkatsina is an Antelope katsina, appearing singly with the mixed katsina dance or with a group of Deer katsinam during Angk'wa, or the summer katsina day dances. The dance is a prayer for the increase of game animals and for successful hunting to supply Hopi with nourishment. The middle Tsivkatsina shows the oldest carving style of the three.*

RIGHT: *From left to right: 1) Pangwu or Pangkatsina is a Big-Horn Sheep katsina, appearing during Angk'wa either with a herd of Pangkatsinam or singly with the mixed katsina group. 2) Honkatsina is a Bear katsina.*

OPPOSITE: *Kawaykatsina is a Horse katsina, one of many animal katsinam. They appear during Angk'wa as a group or singly with the mixed katsina group during the summer katsina day dances. He began to appear after the Spanish brought horses among the Hopi. His songs are prayers for rain and green pastures for animals.*

ABOVE: *From left to right: 1) Kwewu is a Wolf katsina appearing with other animal katsinam, such as the Wakaskatsinam, acting as a herder or a guard. 2–3) Mosayurkatsinam are Buffalo katsinam, appearing during Angk'wa. They appear in pairs with two maidens when the buffalo dance is being performed. Otherwise, they appear singly with the mixed katsina group. The doll on the right is an older Mosayurkatsina.*

OPPOSITE: *Tokotsi or Tokotskatsina is a Wildcat katsina. He appears singly with the mixed katsina group during Angk'wa. His prayers are for rain, and for wildcats to increase in number so their pelts can be used by the Hopi.*

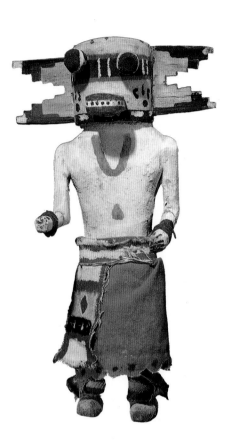

Honankatsina is a Badger katsina, and appears during Angk'wa or the summer katsina day dances. He provides the herbal medicine and represents the medicinal culture, and also serves as a messenger for rain.

Sikyatsungtaqa is known on Second Mesa as Susuk'holi. They are both messengers to the rain gods for the Hopi. They appear during Angk'wa and the summer katsina day dances. They get their name because of the markings on their mouths, and also because of the arrangement of feathers worn as a headdress. This is a Second Mesa Susuk'holi.

Sikyatsuntaqakatsinam (Third Mesa) are rain messengers to rain gods. Their songs are about rainstorms and good life for all mankind.

ABOVE: *Left to right: 1–3) Hololokatsinam are related to the Muuyawu (Moon)
katsina. They appear with various head and
body decorations. Their name is derived
from the sounds they make. 4) Muuyawkatsina is a Moon katsina, a spirit from outer
space. Muuyawu is an important deity in
the Hopi religion, a spirit who guards people
at night and provides special lunar messages
for phases of Hopi ceremonies.*

OPPOSITE: *Kokopölö is a humpback
katsina fertility spirit being. There are
various types, all representing fertility. The
Kokopölökatsina appears during Angk'wa.
These two bring seeds of various plants and
crops, which are stored in their "hump-
backs."*

ABOVE: *Ma'lo is an old, traditional Hopi katsina appearing during Angk'wa, either in a group of Mama'lotu or singly with the mixed katsina group.*

OPPOSITE: *Ma'lo belongs to the early period of katsina development among the Hopi. He performs a dance that portrays a prayer for rain and good crop yield.*

Paalölöqangkatsina is a Water Serpent, appearing during Angk'wa or the summer katsina day dances singly with the mixed katsina group. The songs and sounds of this katsina are prayers for rain.

OPPOSITE: *Manang'yakatsina is a Chameleon katsina who appears in different brilliant colors, representing beauty. In fact, young unmarried men pray to him in hope of finding a beautiful maiden for a wife. These katsinam are usually decorated with the different colors of chameleons on their foreheads, and another is usually carried between the lips. They are also messengers to the rain gods.*

TOP RIGHT: *Tangaktsina is a Rainbow katsina. His headdress is a series of rainbows, each rainbow pointed in four different directions. He appears singly with the mixed katsina group. He is a rain god messenger.*

BOTTOM RIGHT: *Left to right: These are flat katsina dolls, which are usually the very first doll received by female infants. 1) Hanomana is an unmarried katsina maiden of the Hano village of First Mesa. 2) Mongwu is a Great-Horned Owl who appears singly with the mixed katsina group. 3) Hahay'iwuuti is one of the katsina Mothers. 4) Salakmana is a tall and slender katsina maiden.*

Left to right: 1 & 3) Morivoskatsinam are Bean katsinam. They bring various types of beans and represent the moisture for the bean planting season. 2 & 4) Ngayayataqa katsinam are rain messengers who dance in a swaying motion. The name is derived from their style of dancing.

Hoolikatsinam appear as different types of holy katsinam. These are the Kwarurnakvuhooli,
who have eagle tail feathers in place of ears. They are messengers to the rain gods. They appear
during Angk'wa and the summer katsina day dances. The doll on the left is older.

Left to right: All of these katsinam belong to the Ho'tem family, and all are messengers to the rain gods. (Ho'te is singular and Ho'tem is plural). 1 & 3) Qömuvho'tem appear during Angk'wa and the summer katsina day dances. The doll on the left is older. 2) Sakwaho'te is the Uncle of the mixed katsina group and dances to the side, guarding the katsinam. 4) Si'oho'te is a katsina spirit from Zuni Pueblo.

The Hehey'akatsinam are also messengers to the rain gods, as depicted by the cloud symbols on their faces. The one on the far right is the Uncle who dances alongside, guarding the other dancers. He also talks "backwards." If he says "the dance was not a good entertainment," he actually means that the dance was perfect.

Left to right: 1) Hospowi is a Roadrunner katsina. He is a positive symbol for pleasant life. 2) Pawikya is a Duck katsina. 3 & 4) Tootsakatsina is a Hummingbird katsina representing the flourishing of crops and blooming of the earth's plants. The doll on the left (3) is older.

Payik'ala is a Three-Horned katsina.
(Paayom means "three" and ala means
"horn"). He is a messenger to the rain gods
and appears in number during Angk'wa or
singly with the mixed katsina group.

A more recent Payik'ala clearly detailing the
markings of his ceremonial dress.

ABOVE: *Hootsanikatsina is an old Hopi katsina who very seldom dances anymore. He may appear in a group or singly with the mixed katsina group.*

OPPOSITE: *Korososta represents seeds of different plants, especially the crops known to the Hopi. The Korososta katsina brings seeds for the people, and his dances represent "planting." He appears during Angk'wa when planting is beginning.*

Hewtomana, a female katsina who accompanies Hewtokatsinam and related katsina groups, such as the Tsa'kwynakatsinam and Tsitsinom. These katsina groups usually dance during Angk'wa since they bring cold moisture. Hewtomana can also appear singly with the mixed katsina group or separately during the Powamuya ceremony. She sings a special prayer for all mankind.

Tsa'kwynakatsina is a Warrior appearing during Powamuya ceremony and Angk'wa.
Tsa'kwyna spirits represent cold moisture. The katsina doll on the left is the Uncle, a side
dancer with body paints of different colors.

Nuvaktsina is a Snow katsina. He represents cold moisture. He is a friendly katsina who appears during Angk'wa in March and singly with the mixed katsina group during the summer katsina day dances.

EARLY SPRING

KWIYAMUYA

During the season called *Kwiyamuya* (around April), fruit trees begin
to bud, some peach trees are in blossom, and weeds begin to appear
in the cornfields. It is time to prepare and plant gardens and fields
with various crops, especially early corn—*tawaktsi* (sweet corn),
wiqktö (violet corn) and *takurqa'ö* (yellow corn)—and to build *kwiya*
(windbreaks) to protect the seedlings. This period gets its name from
the construction of the windbreaks.

Women are busy shelling corn harvested last year, to be planted
by their sons-in-law, and preparing cornmeal for the upcoming katsina dances as well as other ceremonies. In this busy domestic time,
the *Hototöm* (lean and wiry Racer katsinam) appear in the plazas ges-
turing their desire to challenge the village men and boys to footraces.
A *Koyemsi* (Mudhead katsina) serves as their *mongwi* (chief) and
carries prizes wrapped in a blanket: baked sweet corn and various
breads made of cornmeal. He announces ritually and loudly that the
racer katsinam have brought blessings for a strong and healthy life
and want to test the villagers' strength. The men and boys line up in
single file to take turns racing the katsinam the length of the plaza,
about one hundred yards.

Some of the men and boys are intercepted by two *Kokopölmanavitu* (female fertility beings) who force them to the ground and
make copulatory motions, symbolically promoting the procreation of
life. The paternal aunts who are present in the plaza run to the
Kokopölmanavitu, throw them off, and ridicule them for selecting
and picking on their nephews (paternal aunts are ever-protective of
their nephews.) All this mayhem is accompanied by much laughter
in the plaza. Once the prizes of food are gone, each Racer katsina
selects one person, whom he takes to the starting line for a special
race. Invariably the Racer katsina, with the help of the Kokopölmanavitu, catches the person and takes him to each home in the plaza
where each clan mother of the house pours water on him. He then
receives a variety of items brought by the Racer katsina himself. This
is repeated until each selected man and boy has competed. Finally,
the Koyemsi carefully chooses one individual, presents him with a
qa'öwiki (string of corn) and tells him, in a voice loud enough for all
to hear, when the Racer katsinam will again come to compete.

This cycle is repeated for each kiva in the village and can therefore extend through the entire month of April. The coming of the racers has two purposes: to bless the people and to encourage them to begin training for long- and short-distance running. Tough races are an important part of the upcoming activities in the ceremonial calendar.

The Hototöm are Racer katsinam who appear to challenge the village men and boys to footraces. They also bring blessings for strong and healthy life. Left to right: 1) Patsootskatsina is a Cockleburr Racer katsina. He rubs several cockleburrs into the hair of his opponents when he catches them. 2) Nana'tsuvsikyavo is a Racer katsina who does not boast about his strength. He is a humble challenger, but he always wins. His bright yellow eyes give him strength. 3) Navantsitsiklawqa is a Racer katsina who tears his opponents' shirts when he catches them.

ABOVE: *Left to right: 1) Koyemsi is a Mudhead katsina. He is the leader of the Racers and carries prizes in a wrapped blanket. He ritually challenges a villager's strength. 2) Letotovi is a Mosquito Racer katsina. He sharply whips his opponents: the blows feel like mosquito bites. 3) Kokopölmana is a female Racer katsina who intercepts men and boys and forces them to the ground, making copulatory gestures to promote the procreation of life. 4) Koona is a Chipmunk Racer katsina who is very fast on his feet. His opponents usually are no match for the speedy animal.*

LEFT: *A Koyemsi has selected a spectator and challenges him to a traditional "shinny" game. A small ball is batted back and forth by the players who control and defend it with body and legs, often battering each other's shins. This game can be played by teams of several players and can take several minutes to complete.*

Left to right: 1) Sivutotovi is a Blackfly Racer katsina whose name derives from the fact that his body is all black. He carries a short yucca whip for whipping his opponents. The whip lash resembles the "sting" one might feel when bitten by a fly. 2 & 4) Kokopölmaman't are female Racer katsinam who intercept the opponents and make copulatory gestures to promote the procreation of life. The doll on the left (2) is older. 3) Aykatsina is a Rattle Racer katsina. The designs on each side of the head represent the world. 5) Sivukwewtaqa is a katsina who wears black body paint around his waist.

ABOVE: *Left to right: 1) Malatsvetaqa is a Handprint Racer katsina. He uses soot mixed with grease to leave his handprint on his opponents. 2 & 3) Sösö'pa is the Cricket Racer katsina who whips his opponents gently with a yucca shoot. The doll on the left (2) is older. 4) Hömsona is a Black-Faced Racer katsina who snips a crop of his opponent's hair, especially when a person is wearing a hömsomi (traditional hairstyle with a "bun"). 5) Kiisa is a Chicken Hawk Racer katsina who is very fast. He carries a maawiki (stuffed whip) to whip his opponents with when he catches them.*

OPPOSITE: *Malatsvetaqa is a Handprint Racer katsina. He puts his mark of a handprint on the backs of his opponents. He is wearing his full ceremonial dress, signifying that he has come to perform a dance, which usually takes place when the final racing visits are completed.*

EARLY PLANTING (PÖMA'UYIS)

HAKITONMUYA AND/OR HATIK'UYIS

Crucial to the art of dry farming is knowing the precise planting seasons for various crops. The *Hakitonmuya* period, also called *Hatik'uyis*, is the season for planting *morivosi* (beans) and other vine crops such as *paatnga* (pumpkin), *kawayo* (watermelon), *melooni* (muskmelon) and *tawiya* (gourd). The word *haki* means "wait," and in May it is time to wait for warmer weather before planting corn in large quantities.

All Hopis, except for the very young, are involved in this season's ceremonial and domestic activities, with duties clearly distributed among women and men. Men tend to crops and livestock, weave, hunt large and small game, and perform all major ceremonial responsibilities. Women prepare food both for their families and for ceremonies to insure that their clan children receive proper nourishment. They gather the raw materials for baskets and pottery and support their male clan members in ceremonial duties. For women, a great deal of time is spent in preparing corn for *ngumni* (finely ground cornmeal)—by shelling, winnowing, washing, rough-graining, dry-roasting and fine-grinding corn on *mata* (grinding stones). The finely ground ngumni is then made into a multitude of breads and foods including *piki* (a very thin blue cornmeal bread), *pik'ami* (sweet corn pudding), *somiviki* (corn pudding wrapped in corn husk), and many others.

In May, men of different clans go forth to collect eaglets and young hawks and adopt them into their clan families. The Hopi believe that anything young, like the eaglets, is innocent and pure of heart, thus possessing the greatest spiritual powers. Treated the same as newborn Hopi children, the eaglets receive ritual blessings, have their "hair" washed, and are given a Hopi *tungni* (surname). The name they receive will be in accordance with the clan that adopts them. The eaglets remain within the village to live with and observe the people of the village. In many such ways, by example and recitation of oral history, the Hopi culture is continuously being passed on even during Hatik'uyis as it leads into the next part of the ceremonial calendar, *Wuko'uyis*.

Poos'humkatsina is a Seed katsina. The ceremonial season is embarking on the planting season, and katsinam will be called upon to help with the sprouting and growing of plant life, especially the crops. Markings on each side of the face represent different colors of corn.

Poos'humkatsina, a Seed katsina, usually appears during spring when fields are being prepared for planting. The Poos'humkatsina brings seeds of all kinds, which have been blessed by the supernatural beings, for people to plant. Corn is sacred; it is life; it is Hopi.

ABOVE: *Avatshoya is a White Corn katsina representing excellent crop yield and eventually a bountiful harvest. He is regarded as an Uncle and dances to the side of the single line of katsinam.*

OPPOSITE: *Sootantaqa is another Corn katsina. His name is derived from the conspicuous forward motions he makes, "sootanta" (poking or prodding).*

Qa'ökatsina is a Corn katsina. Sacred corn is very important to the Hopi, for it means life. This katsina carries an ear of corn, which is taken from him by the spectators to be used for planting.

Hopi'avatshoya is a Corn katsina, an original and uniquely Hopi katsina. The circles on the body represent different types of corn, and the white and black band above the forehead represents clouds and rain needed for the corn crops.

ABOVE: *Koyemsi is a Mudhead katsina portraying many personalities from leader to clown. Among them are the "singer" Koyemsimu who sing to different groups of katsinam such as the Avatshoymuy and Hiililimuy. The singer groups bring different poos'humi (seeds) and other gifts, which they carry in the sacks as depicted here. They also bring much humor to the spectators. The doll on the right is older.*

OPPOSITE: *Marawkatsinam represent moisture and are messengers to the rain gods. The katsinam that appear during the summer katsina day dances are friendly, as opposed to the Whippers who appear during Powamuya ceremony. Their conspicuous behavior speaks of their important intermediary function of carrying Hopi prayers to the rain gods and other supernatural beings. The Marawkatsina on the right wants to attract attention by proudly displaying his friendly disposition.*

Navankatsina is a Velvet-Shirt katsina representing the blooming of plant life and focusing on the beauty of life, as indicated by the flowers on his forehead. The Navankatsina is very colorful and his songs are prayers for rain to sustain life. The doll on the right is slightly older.

ABOVE: *Puutskohu is a Rabbit Stick katsina. He brings the art of hunting and represents the increase in game animals for life nourishment. The design on his face is a rabbit stick, a "boomerang"-type object used to hunt rabbits and small game.*

OPPOSITE: *Qa'ökatsina or Ngayayataqa is a Corn katsina representing different types of sacred corn. He dances with a "swaying" motion. The design on his face represents clouds and rain.*

Omawkatsina is the Cumulus Cloud katsina representing rain clouds and summer cloud bursts, which help plant life grow, and replenish sacred springs. He appears with great dignity.

ABOVE: *Left to right: 1–4) Angaktsina is a Longhair katsina, a Rain god. His long hair with eagle fluffs for decoration and his "beard," also decorated with cloud symbols and eagle fluffs, represent cloud bursts or rain. Dolls 1 & 3 are older. 5) Takurmana is a Yellow Corn maiden who also represents rain. These katsinam are favorites among the Hopi. Their songs generally carry positive messages about life.*

LEFT: *Koo'aakatsina is an old Hopi katsina representing rain, as symbolized by the cloud symbols on his forehead. He wears eagle fluffs on top of his head, which represent clouds. The two dolls on the left are slightly older.*

OPPOSITE: *Koo'aakatsina wears a ceremonial kilt and rain sash with cloud symbols.*

ABOVE: *There are Hopi versions of katsinam that honor and depict other tribes, such as the Navajo, Havasupai, Comanche, Zuni and other Pueblos. These are the Hopi versions of what the Navajo katsinam might look like. These katsinam are not* borrowed *from the Navajo, as the katsinam are unique to the Pueblo Indians. They have the same purpose and functions as all the Hopi katsinam: They are messengers and/or intermediaries to the rain gods. Since they are katsinam in every respect, they are afforded the same reverence and dignity during their visits. The Tasavkatsinam in the photo represent two male-female pairs. The males are wearing ceremonial kilts and have blue faces and red hair; the females are wearing prescribed cere-monial clothing with their hair in a traditional style. They appear during Angk'wa and the summer katsina day dances. Since they are depicting the Navajo, their songs may have some Navajo words speaking of the good things of life and/or words representing moisture. They dance at a slow pace with a twisting movement, the male singing in a low, deep voice while the female sings in a high-pitched voice. They are messengers to the rain gods.*

Yé'ii Bicheii is a Tasavkatsina, though much different than the ones at left or on page 81. These appear in a group, dancing at a fast pace to the singing of a group of Navajo katsina singers. They are messengers to the rain gods, and receive much reverence during their visit to the Hopi.

OPPOSITE, TOP: *This photo depicts yet another form of Navajo katsinam, called the Kwivikatsinam, meaning "showy." Their ceremonial dress is flashy, attracting a lot of attention. They wear brightly colored ribbons on their headdresses and their kilts, making their appearance very attractive. At the far right is Tonaylili (small river), the Uncle who dances on the side, making arm and hand motions to echo the meaning of the song. He, too, is attractively dressed.*

Yé'ii Bicheii is the Navajo katsina Grandfather. He appears with the Tasavkatsinam, dancing on the side, making arm and hand motions depicting the meaning of the song. He assists the katsina chief in taking care of the katsinam. The Yé'ii Bicheii dresses in the traditional Navajo ceremonial wear, using the white buckskin as a cape. He has a corn plant painted on his face, representing a good crop yield and a bountiful harvest. These are older, traditional Yé'ii Bicheii katsina dolls.

BOTTOM: *Koninkatsinam depict the Havasupai tribe, which resides at the bottom of the Grand Canyon. The photo shows the male members of the katsinam. Left to right: 1 & 3) These two Koninkatsinam are usually accompanied by Konin maidens during the dance, which is in a single line, alternating male and female. 2) The Uncle dances to the side. Koninkatsinam are very colorful, appearing during Angk'wa and the summer katsina day dances. Their songs are about moisture in the form of rain, with references to the taking of the mule deer bucks, the suta (red sienna), buckskins, and kwaani (dried figs), all of which they traded with the Hopi.*

PLANTING SEASON

Wuko'uyis

Wuko'uyis (June planting season) is an important time for all plant life, especially the sacred corn, which receives the special blessing of rain to support its growth to maturity.

Traditionally, a clan mother sponsors an *uuaya'ta* (organized planting party) in her clan cornfield. She visits each of her *mööyi* (paternal nephews) and asks them, in a sincere manner, to assist their *kyamuy* (paternal aunts) and *so'oh* (paternal grandmother) in the cornfield. The request is taken as an honor and accepted graciously. The next day all the clan nephews, young and old, show up in the field with their *sooya* (planting sticks) to plant various kinds and colors of corn, accompanied by a great deal of teasing and good-natured fun. This time is also used to teach the young children the art of dry farming. Afterward, everyone is rewarded with a feast of several kinds of *nöqkwivi* (stew), and *noova* (bread and pastry).

By now, people who live near the kiva have heard the sounds of katsina songs in the nights. Throughout the season the katsinam will appear in all twelve Hopi villages, sometimes at several villages on the same day. Excitement spreads from one village to another as people await the first day of the *tiikive* (dance). The male members of the village who are initiated in the katsina rituals visit the kiva to smoke ceremonially, meditate, and pray for plentiful crops.

On the day before the dance, preparations intensify, men engaging in ceremonial functions, women assisting with ceremonial support and the preparation of food.

Precisely at sunrise on the dance day, the katsinam physically appear and proceed in single file to the plaza, bringing gifts of good fortune, virtue, and moisture for all plant life.

Encouraged by the kiva chief, with the shake of a rattle the katsinam begin their rhythmic dancing, singing their loud, mesmerizing prayer-song while bells jingle, turtle shells clatter, and drums pulse. At midday, the katsinam are served sacred food by the women. Throughout the day the katsinam pause to bestow gifts of food to the people—samples of what the harvest will eventually bring in plenty.

Mongwu is a Great-Horned Owl who plays a significant role in bringing the Whipper katsinam to punish the clowns during the summer katsina day dances. The Mongwu plays the role of a sorcerer, jointly planning with the chief clown, in secrecy, the punishment attack of the clowns.

The photo depicts several types of clown katsinam. Left to right: 1) This Tsuku is a Second Mesa (Musangnuvi/Supawlavi) Clown. He is painted all yellow, with red stripes of suta (red sienna) across his face. 3) This Tsuku is a Third Mesa Clown. 2, 4 & 5) Koyaala are Clowns from the Hano village of First Mesa. They are white with black horizontal stripes around their bodies and black markings over their eyes and mouths. The Koyaala katsinam are singers to the Deer and Big-Horned Sheep katsinam. Their actions bring much humor to the spectators. The human counterparts of the Koyaala are caretakers of the katsinam during the summer katsina day dances. They are the rowdy type who poke fun at the people and katsina clowns, and who are punished for their mischievous behavior by the Whipper katsinam.

At about noon, a rowdy handful of human clowns appear on the roof of one of the plaza houses and make their raucous and awkward way down, in search of the katsinam. The clowns have a very complex ceremonial role. They act out many activities indicative of that which is not in keeping with the Hopi way—dishonesty, disrespectfulness, laziness. In doing so they provide a great deal of amusement for the people. Their acts provide serious and wise advice, for the clowns also personify the days of childhood when one is pure of heart. They are a spiritually powerful critic of unacceptable behavior. The clowns, emphasizing positive lessons by performing negative acts, are thus more like sacred priests than mere clowns. They are honored by great quantities of food (which they feast upon right there in the plaza) and they are, indeed, considered the caretakers of the katsinam.

At sunset, the dance concludes with loud prayers and blessings as the katsinam and the clowns depart the plaza. If the dance sponsors wish the katsinam to perform again the next day, they are so informed, and are led by the kiva chief and the clowns to the sponsoring kiva, where they will remain through the night until midmorning the next day.

When the katsinam return, they continue their dancing, prayers, and meditations, much like the day before, until sunset. Reluctantly, the katsinam are sent home to their spirit world and silence falls on the plaza as the katsina dance comes to a peaceful and devout close.

Tseveyo is an Ogre katsina who also plays a significant role during the summer katsina day dances. His function is that of a disciplinarian. His actions and speech represents enforcement and the maintenance of order. He disciplines people if their conduct or behavior is not practiced according to the accepted standards. He also appears during Powamuya ceremony with the Whipper katsinam, or during Angk'wa with the mixed katsina group. When requested, he appears on special occasions to maintain order, such as the summer katsina day dances when clowns are being disorderly.

SUMMER SOLSTICE SEASON

TALANGVA

Talangva is summer (July) and all the activities of summer climax
with the sacred Niman ceremony, an important ritual ending the
katsina season. In the Niman ceremony, the katsinam who have
been on the earth in their physical form since the winter solstice will
return home to their spiritual world. Plant life has now blossomed in
acknowledgement of the people's prayers and meditations, the
powerful energy of the katsina blessings, and the participation of
the supernatural beings in the cycle of ceremonies from November
through June.

NIMANKATSINA CEREMONY

The Niman ceremony is performed precisely at midsummer. It is the
time of the most intense prayer and meditation in the village. In the
sponsoring kiva, the kiva chief and the priesthood leaders conduct
rituals. All are for the benefit of all mankind. As the villagers look
forward to their *totokya* (a period of days surrounding a dance), even
the eagles' noisy squawking and wing-flapping seem to intensify the
seriousness of the season.

At sunrise on the day of the dance, the Hemiskatsinam appear at
the plaza bearing stalks of corn and melons. This symbolically represents that they have brought their bounty and the intangible virtues
of life for the people. At some of the villages, other katsinam now
perform the Niman ceremony. With stately elegance and dignified
mannerisms, the katsinam are accompanied by the *katsinmamantu*
(katsina maidens). The maidens are costumed in finely woven and
embroidered dresses, their hair arranged in the butterfly whorls that
indicate they are unmarried. The majestic appearance of these pretty
maidens provides the spectators with the pervading spirit of maternal
idealism. As the katsinam dance throughout the day, the katsinmamantu compliment the dancing and singing with their own musi-
cal instruments. At the onset of the last dance, the village's brides of
that year are presented, dressed in their wedding robes, to receive
special blessings from the katsinam and other supernatural beings. To
symbolize these blessings for ideal motherhood, each bride receives
an elaborately created katsina doll. It is a special day for the brides.

The groom's mother will *tiimayna* (present) the bride to the spirits. The bride will one day join the spirits in life after death, for she will be buried in the *ovaa* (wedding robe) she is wearing.

At the end of the last dance, the spirits will depart this earth and return to the spirit world, carrying the special prayers of the Hopi to the six directions of the Hopi world.

The next morning, the katsinam perform their final ritual of the ceremonial cycle. Life is thus purified. The katsinam return to the world of spirit. The eagles too must now accompany them, bearing prayers and their own observations of the events that have taken place during their stay in the village.

The Hopi katsina season comes to a peaceful close.

The Niman ceremony (Home Dance) in July is an important katsina ceremony. That is when the katsinam return to their spiritual homes for about a six-month period. Their role of support for the growth of plant life, especially the early corn, has been completed and consecrated. Left to right:
2) Hemiskatsina is a Nimankatsina who carries out this important dance accompanied by katsina maidens of several types.
1 & 3) Katsinmanavitu are katsina maidens. They are very pretty, wearing their hairstyle in butterfly whorls, a traditional hairstyle of Hopi maidens.

Qötsamanavitu are Snow maidens who also accompany the Hemiskatsinam during Niman ceremony. The Hemiskatsinam sing in low, deep voices, while the katsina maidens sing in high-pitched voices, each beautifully complementing the other. There are two parts to the dance: the second part requires the maidens to kneel and play their gourd/rasp rain-makers. Their songs are in themselves prayers for rain and eventually a bountiful harvest. The Ewtoto, the katsina priest of a high order, again appears with three Hemiskatsinam, or sometimes two Hemiskatsinam and a maiden. The Ewtoto leads the katsinam in the blessing ceremony. Once their ritual is completed and consecrated, they are sent home, symbolic of the katsinam going to their spiritual homes.

ABOVE: There are different types of Nimankatsinam. Si'ohemiskatsina (left) is a Zuni katsina shown with his katsina maiden, the Hohomana. Hohomana is still another katsina maiden who appears with the Hemiskatsinam.

OPPOSITE: Left to right: Si'ohemiskatsina (Zuni) and the Nimankatsina (Hopi). The two Hemiskatsinam together show excellent contrast.

ABOVE: *The Ewtoto (left) leads the Hemis-katsinam (middle) and/or katsinmana (right) a day after the Niman ceremony to perform formal rituals that are completed before the katsinam are symbolically sent to their spiritual homes.*

RIGHT: *Maasawkatsina is an Earth god, the only type of katsina to remain on Hopi for the entire year.*

This Maasawkatsina is holding a flat cradle doll, which is given to an infant.

Maasawkatsinmana is a maiden who accompanies the Maasawkatsinam. She appears during Angk'wa, and the summer katsina day dances, and after the Niman ceremony, when the katsinam have gone to their spiritual home. The Maasawkatsinam dance is somewhat like the Hemiskatsinam, with the maidens using their gourd/rasp rain-makers as a prayer for moisture. These katsinam bring gifts of nat'wani (different crops), and different breads made of cornmeal. Their specialty is the bread called koletviki, a bread of blue cornmeal baked over the piki-stone. They represent protection and guidance, moisture of rain, and bountiful harvest.

TOP: *These katsinam are very seldom seen in public because their performance of rituals is sacred and secret, reserved only for specific clans or high priesthood leaders. Left to right: 1 & 3) Tawakatsina, a handsome spirit being, is very popular among the doll carvers, but he very seldom appears in the katsina dances. The doll on the right (3) is slightly older. 2) Qa'ötorikiwtaqa is a katsina who represents corn. He wears two strings of different colors of corn around his shoulders, sometimes crossed diagonally over his shoulders.*

BOTTOM: *Hohotaqa is the male spirit related to the Hohomana, a katsina maiden who accompanies the Hemiskatsina during the Niman ceremony. The name* Hoho *is derived from the sounds he makes as he journeys about in the universe. He is an old Hopi katsina who very seldom appears.*

LEFT: *Owaktsinam are Coal katsinam who represent the minerals and their beneficial values for the people. These are also old Hopi katsinam who very seldom appear.*

RIGHT: *Wukoqalakatsinam are Big-Forehead katsinam. There are at least two types of Big-Forehead katsinam, these being of the older type. It is believed that these katsinam are borrowed from the Zuni Pueblo.*

SUMMER SOCIAL DANCES

TALA'PAAMUYA

When people are peacefully recollecting pleasant memories of the katsina season, giving thanks to the *Nimankatsinmuy* for their special blessings and the bringing of the early corn and other crops, it is time for the Flute and Snake-Antelope ceremonies, held on alternate years. The purpose of these ceremonies is to bring the last summer rains to insure the maturity of corn and other crops before harvest, and to prepare the fields for the next planting season.

An underground ceremonial chamber, or kiva, on one of the Hopi villages.

SUMMER SOCIAL DANCES

In late summer (last part of August and first part of September) the plaza may again fill with colorful dancers, young and unmarried women and their *mööyi,* (paternal nephews) performing one of many social dances. Most common and perhaps the most colorful is the butterfly dance. These are non-katsina ceremonies. There are also dances that honor other tribes such as Navajo, Havasupai, Supai, Zuni, and Comanche. Like the earlier dances of winter, these are carefully choreographed and rehearsed for several nights in the kiva.

The couples, dancing in unison, create a pleasant, hypnotic sight for the spectators. They are accompanied by some twenty men singing in full voice whose gestures (a kind of sign language) echo the meaning of the song, itself a prayer for good things for all people. In the excitement of the dance, Hopi women from the crowd will often rush in and select their nephews from the group of singing men and join the long single-file line of dancers that fill the plaza.

All the women who dance, including those who take the sons of their male relatives from the group of singers, must give their partners noova. In turn, the men must give them *sikwi* (wild game meat). While these social activities are carried out with a great deal of teasing and good-natured fun among the clan relatives, the dances are also quasi-religious events, formal and public expressions of gratitude for ample crops and for life in general. According to Hopi belief, a public event such as this, in which gratitude is expressed freely and openly, is the most powerful way to focus the people's energy to accomplish the mission of the ceremony. For that reason no one in the Hopi community is ever excluded from watching these dances and offering their own prayers.

HARVEST SEASON

NASANMUYA

For the Hopi, the harvest season in September is consecrated by a
women's ceremony, the *Marawwimi* (one of three women's societies). Only women who have completed their initiation into the
Maraw society are eligible to perform the dance itself. Other ceremonial activities are performed by men initiated into the Maraw society.
Both men and women initiated into the society consecrate the
prayers and meditations.

*The Hopi people practice the art of dry farm-
ing, meaning they depend on rain and snow
moisture for their crops to grow. Katsina
spirits are called upon to carry prayers for
rain to the rain gods for a bountiful harvest
of different crops.*

WINTER SOLSTICE SEASON

TOHO'OSMUYA

The *Lakon* ceremony, the second in the cycle of women's ceremonies, is held in *Toho'osmuya* (October). The ceremony itself expresses the desire for healthy impregnation and reinforces maternal ideals. It is commonly referred to as a Basket Dance, and is equal in importance to the *O'waqölt* (below). Only the women who have completed an initiation into the Lakon society can participate in the ceremony. With their initiation into this society, women also learn the art of weaving of different types of colorful baskets. While the ceremony is performed primarily by women, other ceremonial requirements are carried out by *Lakontataqtu* (men who are initiated into the Lakon society). The meditations and prayers are collectively consecrated by all the participants, men and women.

O'WAQÖLT (BASKET DANCE)

The *O'waqölt* is another important series of women's ceremonies conducted during this season. The ceremonial mission is similar to that of the other women ceremonies in that it expresses the concept of healthy impregnation and reinforces maternal idealism. The dance is performed by women, while other important ceremonial aspects are carried out by men. All the participants, men and women, collectively consecrate the ceremony through meditations and prayers.

The ceremonial calendar ends with the completion of the ceremonial rituals and dances conducted by the women's religious societies. It is again time to formalize and decree the next year's colorful and festive Hopi ceremonial calendar.

OPPOSITE: *Colorful coiled plaques, which the women weave, are unique to Hopi. The designs vary, focusing attention on the beauty of earth and its useful resources. They also serve as a reminder that humans are caretakers of Mother Earth.*

CONCLUSION

The Hopi are perhaps the most religious and spiritual people in the world. Their comprehensive and extensive involvement in religious affairs preoccupies most of their time and thoughts. Their participation in religious ceremonies and rituals; creation and production of art work, such as textile weaving and embroidery, basketry, pottery, silversmithing, and katsina dolls; farming occupation; pilgrimages to the shrines that monument their traditional land use area; gathering of objects and plants for ceremonial and medicinal uses, and herbs for food savory qualities; and the clanship of these important, riteful things-in-themselves complement the religious mission in securing life blessings for the benefit of all mankind. Accordingly, when the Hopi offer prayers to the supernatural beings, they ask for things much greater than their own well-being.

The question "What is a Hopi?" is often asked by many people, including the Hopi people themselves. Based on my life experiences, I believe restraint and self-control are valued and are considered important virtues of the Hopi way of life. Because self-respect is essential to a Hopi, it is expected each will respect another person as highly as he does himself. Individual behavior is guided by strict rules of decency. In summary, self-respect is the principle applied in the social, political, and religious structures of the Hopi, constituting the great virtues of humbleness and peace.

Owen Seumptewa

A young girl holding the katsina doll that was given to her by the Hennikatsinam at the Niman ceremony.

APPENDIX A: HOPILAND VISITOR INFORMATION

Many individuals can make positive and meaningful contributions to another people and their way of life.

Through all we have seen and experienced as the Hopi people, many Hopi have come to perceive an important involvement for ourselves in managing vital issues and technological changes that will have direct influence on our way of life, religion, and culture. Challenges have been numerous in the past. The external forces of the twentieth century, particularly the outside religions, have had a major impact. However, we believe our greatest bond has been our religious teachings and practices; they have given us the strength to minimize the effects of these strong external forces. They have provided processes for cooperation and respect for people generally, and have kept us united for time immemorial. We are a peace-loving, closely knit clan with extended families: an intensely spiritual and independent people. We also, I believe, have much to offer to our guests and can learn things of value from them as well.

To insure that your visit to Hopiland is a pleasant experience as well as a meaningful and a memorable one, we provide some general remarks and guidelines.

Many religious and cultural activities are closed to visitors. Do not attempt to observe any activity you have not received permission to attend. Those that you may be permitted to witness are not for entertainment. All Hopi ceremonies are highly spiritual in content and should be viewed and respected as such. As with all deeply religious activities in any culture, it requires extensive preparation to accomplish the religious and ceremonial mission. Hopi philosophy teaches that life is very special and important, and that each person must be given an opportunity to offer heartfelt prayers during public viewing of these spiritual events. This is the most spiritually powerful way to focus the people's energies to accomplish the ceremonial mission. Accordingly, guests are expected to show appropriate behavior, respect and courtesy. Your positive influences and prayers will strengthen and benefit all life forms and all things in the world, which is the ceremonial purpose.

Each Hopi village usually has a sign which provides useful information for the visiting tourists. This one is a sign at the entrance to First Mesa Villages.

Proper Attire

Dress neatly and presentably. Women should wear dresses that are at least knee-length, or long pants and blouses. Men should wear long pants and shirts (T-shirts are acceptable). Hats and umbrellas are considered disrespectful. Do not wear shorts. Shoes are required.

Other Guidelines

Photography, sketching, tape-recording, and videotaping are not permitted. If you are caught doing any of these activities, your cameras, video equipment, tape recorders and recording materials will be confiscated, and you will be asked to leave. No one should have to divert their attention from the ceremony to deal with a visitor's disrespectful behavior. Behavior of this type in the past has contributed to the reasons for closure of many ceremonies to non-Indians.

NO ALCOHOLIC BEVERAGES OR ILLEGAL DRUGS ARE PERMITTED ON THE HOPI RESERVATION. Any non-Indian who is caught with alcohol and/or illegal drugs in their possession is subject to Navajo County laws and can be cited by the Justice of the Peace either in Holbrook or Winslow, Arizona. Any major crime committed by anyone (Indian or non-Indian) is subject to federal law and will be prosecuted by the U.S. District Attorney in U.S. District Court.

APPENDIX B:
LIST OF KATSINA DOLLS

COLLECTION INFORMATION

Many donors have contributed katsina dolls to The Heard Museum collection. Several important private collections that were donated to the museum are recognized in this list.

Mr. and Mrs. Dwight Heard's original collection of katsina dolls was fairly small. Approximately 25 dolls are included in the museum's permanent collection, of which a few are Zuni. Some of these dolls were collected prior to the establishment of the museum in 1929.

Goldwater Collection: In 1964, Senator Barry M. Goldwater donated his collection of 437 katsina dolls to The Heard Museum. Some of the older tihu, carved between the late 1800s and 1940, were originally in the collection of architect John Rinker Kibbey.

Fred Harvey Fine Arts Collection: The Fred Harvey Company established its Indian Department in 1902. The department purchased many quality collections for sale in the company's gift shops. Pieces of extraordinary quality were set aside for the company's special collection. In 1978, the Harvey family donated this collection to The Heard Museum.

Fred Harvey/Owen Collection: Collected by C.L. Owen, anthropologist with the Field Museum, Chicago, at Second Mesa in 1911 and 1913.

Fred Harvey/Voth Collection: Collected for the Harvey Company by Mennonite missionary Henry Voth, who lived at Third Mesa and consulted with the Harvey Company on several projects related to Hopi. His collection of katsina dolls for the Harvey Company is thought to have been made in 1903.

Fred Harvey/Volz Collection: The Harvey Company purchased 400 katsina dolls from trader Frederick Volz in 1901. Volz's trading post was at Canyon Diablo near First Mesa, and he began trading with people at Hopi in 1899.

Byron Harvey, III, Collection: The great-grandson of the founder of the Fred Harvey Company, Byron Harvey, developed an impressive collection of Native American arts, primarily during the 1960s, which he donated to The Heard Museum in 1971.

Cover and p. 41
Wakaskatsina
Catalog number: NA-SW-HO-F-327
Height: 11 in.
Date: c. 1900
Goldwater Collection

p. 7
Ahöla (left)
Catalog number: NA-SW-HO-F-503
Carver: Louis C. Honwytewa
Height: 10.5 in.
Date: c. 1970
Byron Harvey, III, Collection

Ahöla (right)
Catalog number: NA-SW-HO-F-434
Height: 14 in.
Date: c. 1960
Goldwater Collection

p. 8
Ahölatmana'at (left)
Catalog number: NA-SW-HO-F-68
Carver: Oswald White Bear Fredericks
Height: 12 in.
Date: c. 1960
Goldwater Collection

Ahölatmana'at (right)
Catalog number: NA-SW-HO-F-61
Carver: Oswald White Bear Fredericks
Height: 13 in.
Date: c. 1960
Goldwater Collection

p.9
Ewtoto (left)
Catalog number: NA-SW-HO-F-749
Height: 12.6 in.
Date: c. 1980
Gift of Mr. and Mrs. Thomas White

Áholi (right)
Catalog number: NA-SW-HO-F-748
Height: 15.25 in.
Date: c. 1980
Gift of Mr. and Mrs. Thomas White

p. 10
Lenangkatsina
Catalog number: 781CI
Height: 12.25 in.
Date: pre-1901
Fred Harvey/Volz Collection

p. 11
Lenangmana
Catalog number: 300CI
Height: 14 in.
Date: pre-1913
Fred Harvey/Owen Collection

p. 12
Awhalayni (left)
Catalog number: NA-SW-HO-F-227
Carver: Oswald White Bear Fredericks
Height: 12 in.
Date: 1960
Goldwater Collection

Awhalayni (right)
Catalog number: NA-SW-HO-F-53
Carver: Oswald White Bear Fredericks
Height: 12.5 in.
Date: 1960
Goldwater Collection

p. 13
Qaletaqa
Catalog number: NA-SW-HO-F-27
Height: 19 in.
Date: 1930s–1940s
Heard Museum Collection

p. 13
Kokosorhoya (left)
Catalog number: 1731CI
Height: 9 in.
Date: 1920s–1940s
Fred Harvey Collection

Sola'wutsi (right)
Catalog number: NA-SW-HO-F-368
Height: 6 in.
Date: c. 1920
Goldwater Collection

p. 17
Angwusnasomtaqa (left)
Catalog number: NA-SW-HO-F-705
Carver: Jim Fred
Height: 17.75 in.
Date: 1984
Museum Purchase

Angwusnasomtaqa (right)
Catalog number: NA-SW-HO-F-20
Height: 9.75 in.
Date: c. 1900
Original Heard Collection

p. 17
Tungwivkatsina (left)
Catalog number: NA-SW-HO-F-274
Height: 11 in.
Date: c. 1920
Goldwater Collection

Tungwivkatsina (left center)
Catalog number: NA-SW-HO-F-89
Height: 12 in.
Date: pre-1900
Goldwater Collection

Tungwivkatsina (center)
Catalog number: 863CI
Height: 12.5 in.
Date: pre-1901
Fred Harvey/Volz Collection

Tungwivkatsina (right center)
Catalog number: 834CI
Height: 12.5 in.
Date: pre-1901
Fred Harvey/Volz Collection

Tungwivkatsina (right)
Catalog number: 854CI
Height: 11 in.
Date: pre-1901
Fred Harvey/Volz Collection

p. 18
Kokopölö
Catalog number: NA-SW-HO-F-493
Height: 15 in.
Date: c. 1970
Byron Harvey, III, Collection

p. 19
Powamuykatsina (left)
Catalog number: 831CI
Height: 9.75 in.
Date: pre-1901
Fred Harvey/Volz Collection

Lenangkatsina (center)
Catalog number: NA-SW-HO-F-506
Carver: Neil David
Height: 9 in.
Date: c. 1970
Byron Harvey, III, Collection

Powamuykatsina (right)
Catalog number: 890CI
Height: 11.75 in.
Date: pre-1901
Fred Harvey/Volz Collection

p. 20
Angwusnasomtaqa
Catalog number: 774CI
Height: 14.5 in.
Date: pre-1901
Fred Harvey/Volz Collection

p. 20
Kwikwilyaqa (left)
Catalog number: NA-SW-HO-F-441
Height: 10 in.
Date: 1969
Museum Purchase

Hiilili (left center)
Catalog number: NA-SW-HO-F-531
Carver: Wayne Taylor
Height: 9 in.
Date: c. 1960s
Byron Harvey, III Collection

Sikyaqöqlo (right center)
Catalog number: NA-SW-HO-F-499
Carver: Marshall Lomakema
Height: 11.5 in.
Date: 1969
Byron Harvey, III, Collection

Sootukwnang (right)
Catalog number: NA-SW-HO-F-537
Carver: Allie Selestewa
Height: 10.5 in.
Date: 1970
Byron Harvey, III, Collection

p. 21
Mastopkatsina (left)
Catalog number: NA-SW-HO-F-175
Height: 11 in.
Date: c. 1950s
Goldwater Collection

Áholi (center)
Catalog number: NA-SW-HO-F-59
Carver: Oswald White Bear Fredericks
Height: 13 in.
Date: c. 1960
Goldwater Collection

Tuvatsqöqlo (right)
Catalog number: NA-SW-HO-F-166
Height: 10.5 in.
Date: 1900–1920
Goldwater Collection

p. 22
Ma'lo (left)
Catalog number: 606CI
Height: 7.75 in.
Date: pre-1913
Fred Harvey/Owen Collection

Sikyaqöqlo (center)
Catalog number: NA-SW-HO-F-718
Carver: Manfred Susunkewa
Height: approx. 9 in.
Date: 1984
Museum Purchase

Hahay'iwuuti (right)
Catalog number: 1176CI
Height: 4.5 in.
Date: c. 1910
Fred Harvey Collection

p. 22
Sipiknitaqa (left)
Catalog number: 835CI
Height: 13.25 in.
Date: c. 1900
Fred Harvey Collection

Sipiknitaqa (right)
Catalog number: 1199CI
Height: 8.75 in.
Date: c. 1900
Fred Harvey Collection

p. 23
Ewizro
Catalog number: 891CI
Height: 12 in.
Date: pre-1901
Fred Harvey Collection/Volz

p. 23
Wupamokatsina (left)
Catalog number: NA-SW-HO-F-462
Carver: Richard J. Pentewa
Height: 15.5 in.
Date: 1970
Museum Purchase

Wupamokatsina (center)
Catalog number: NA-SW-HO-F-689
Carver: Manfred Susunkewa
Height: 11 in.
Date: 1987
Museum Purchase

Wupamokatsina (right)
Catalog number: 855CI
Height: 12.5 in.
Date: pre-1901
Fred Harvey/Volz Collection

p. 24
Muyingwa
Catalog number: NA-SW-HO-F-146
Height: 10 in.
Date: c. 1900
Goldwater Collection

p.25
Tsanayo (left)
Catalog number: NA-SW-HO-F-396
Height: 12 in.
Date: pre-1900
Goldwater Collection

Tsitoto (left center)
Catalog number: NA-SW-HO-F-155
Height: 10 in.
Date: 1900–1920
Goldwater Collection

Kwewu (center)
Catalog number: NA-SW-HO-F-704
Carver: Jimmie Kewanwytewa
Height: 11.75 in.
Date: 1950s
Gift of Dr. W. Storrs Cole

Hiilili (right center)
Catalog number: NA-SW-HO-F-30
Height: 10 in.
Date: 1940s–1952
Heard Museum Collection

Hee'e'e (right)
Catalog number: NA-SW-HO-F-727
Carver: Jimmie Kewanwytewa
Height: 13 in.
Date: c. 1950s
Gift of Dr. W. Storrs Cole

p. 25
Aalosaka
Catalog number: 299CI
Height: 17.5 in.
Date: pre-1913
Fred Harvey/Owen Collection

p. 26
Motsinkatsina (left)
Catalog number: 822CI
Height: 11.25 in.
Date: pre-1901
Fred Harvey/Volz Collection

Motsinkatsina (right)
Catalog number: 832CI
Height: 10.5 in.
Date: pre-1901
Fred Harvey/Volz Collection

p. 27
Kwikwilyaqa
Catalog number: NA-SW-HO-F-445
Height: 13 in.
Date: pre-1969
Museum Purchase

p. 28
Hiilili (left)
Catalog number: NA-SW-HO-F-426
Height: 12 in.
Date: 1940s–1950s
Goldwater Collection

Haaniiya (left center)
Catalog number: 853CI
Height: est. 15 in.
Date: pre-1901
Fred Harvey/Volz Collection

Haaniiya (right center)
Catalog number: NA-SW-HO-F-628
Carver: Peter Shelton
Height: 14.5 in.
Date: early 1960s
Museum Purchase

Hiilili (right)
Catalog number: 844CI
Height: 8.75 in.
Date: pre-1901
Fred Harvey/Volz Collection

p. 29
Sootukwnang (left)
Catalog number: 777CI
Height: 15.25 in.
Date: pre-1901
Fred Harvey/Volz Collection

Hiilili (right)
Catalog number: NA-SW-HO-F-243
Height: 9 in.
Date: 1920s–1930s
Goldwater Collection

p. 29
So'yokwuuti (left)
Catalog number: 3441-7
Carver: Theodore Pavatea
Height: 12 in.
Date: 1993
Museum Purchase

So'yoktaqa (center)
Catalog number: NA-SW-HO-F-293
Height: 10 in.
Date: 1920s–1940s
Goldwater Collection

Tossonkoyemsi (right)
Catalog number: NA-SW-HO-F-495
Height: 13 in.
Date: c. 1970
Byron Harvey, III, Collection

p. 31
Nata'aska
Catalog number: NA-SW-HO-F-126
Height: 18 in.
Date: 1900–1920
Goldwater Collection

p. 32
Nata'aska
Catalog number: NA-SW-HO-F-753
Carver: Brian Honyouti
Height: 18.75 in.
Date: 1990
Museum Purchase

p. 32
Wiharu
Catalog number: NA-SW-HO-F-125
Height: 17 in.
Date: ca. 1900
Goldwater Collection

p. 33
Hehey'a (left)
Catalog number: NA-SW-HO-F-163
Height: 8.5 in.
Date: 1900–1920
Goldwater Collection

Qötsawihazru (right)
Catalog number: NA-SW-HO-F-719
Carver: Henry Shelton
Height: 14.5 in.
Date: 1984
Museum Purchase

p. 35
Palhikmana
Catalog number: 814CI
Height: 13.25 in.
Date: early 1900s
Fred Harvey Collection

p. 37
Poliimana
Catalog number: NA-SW-HO-F-64
Carver: Jimmie Kewanwytewa
Height: 17 in.
Date: 1950s
Goldwater Collection

p. 38
Kyaro (left)
Catalog number: NA-SW-HO-F-116
Carver: Oswald White Bear Fredericks
Height: 12 in.
Date: 1959
Goldwater Collection

Kwahu (left center)
Catalog number: NA-SW-HO-F-228
Height: 8 in.
Goldwater Collection

Tootsa (right center)
Catalog number: NA-SW-HO-F-171
Height: 9.5 in.
Date: 1930s–1940s
Goldwater Collection

Pawikya (right)
Catalog number: NA-SW-HO-F-277
Height: 11 in.
Date: 1900
Goldwater Collection

p. 39
Pootawikkatsina
Catalog number: 847CI
Height: 13 in.
Date: c. 1900
Fred Harvey Collection

p. 40
Kwahu (left)
Catalog number: NA-SW-HO-F-102
Height: 10 in.
Date: 1940s–1950s
Goldwater Collection

Kwahu (center)
Catalog number: NA-SW-HO-F-118
Height: 6 in.
Date: 1950s–1964
Goldwater Collection

Kwahu (right)
Catalog number: NA-SW-HO-F-420
Height: 11 in.
Date: 1950s–1964
Goldwater Collection

p. 41
Wakaskatsina (left)
Catalog number: NA-SW-HO-F-488
Carver: Marshall Lomakema
Height: 15.5 in.
Byron Harvey, III, Collection

Wakaskatsinmana (right)
Catalog number: NA-SW-HO-F-497
Carver: Arnold Taylor
Height: 11 in.
Date: c. 1970
Byron Harvey, III, Collection

p. 42
Kawaykatsina
Catalog number: 1698CI
Height: 11.5 in.
Date: pre-1939
Fred Harvey Collection

p. 43
Tsivkatsina (left)
Catalog number: NA-SW-HO-F-324
Height: 12 in.
Date: c. 1900
Goldwater Collection

Tsivkatsina (center)
Catalog number: NA-SW-HO-F-73
Height: 13 in.
Date: 1900–1920
Goldwater Collection

Tsivkatsina (right)
Catalog number: NA-SW-HO-F-407
Height: 12 in.
Date: 1900–1920
Goldwater Collection

p. 43
Pangwu/Pangkatsina (left)
Catalog number: NA-SW-HO-F-423
Height: 13 in.
Date: 1950s
Goldwater Collection

Honkatsina (right)
Catalog number: NA-SW-HO-F-124
Height: 13 in.
Date: 1950s
Goldwater Collection

p. 44
Kwewu (left)
Catalog number: 1194CI
Height: 12 in.
Date: pre-1903
Fred Harvey/Voth Collection

Mosayurkatsina (center)
Catalog number: NA-SW-HO-F-306
Height: 7 in.
Date: 1940s
Goldwater Collection

Mosayurkatsina (right)
Catalog number: NA-SW-HO-F-347
Height: 10 in.
Date: pre-1900
Goldwater Collection

p. 45
Tokotsi/Tokotskatsina
Catalog number: NA-SW-HO-F-612
Carver: Se-Ona
Height: 10.75 in.
Date: 1975
Gift of Byron Hunter, Jr.

p. 46
Honankatsina
Catalog number: 869CI
Height: 13.25 in.
Date: pre-1901
Fred Harvey/Volz Collection

p. 46
Susuk'holi
Catalog number: NA-SW-HO-F-715
Height: 10.75 in.
Date: 1940s–1950s
Museum Purchase

p. 47
Sikyatsungtaqa
Catalog number: 805CI
Height: 13.25 in.
Date: 1900–1920s
Fred Harvey Collection

p. 48
Hololokatsina (left)
Catalog numbers: NA-SW-HO-F-134
Height: 9 in.
Date: 1900–1920s
Goldwater Collection

Hololokatsina (left center)
Catalog number: 802CI
Height: 15.75 in.
Date: pre-1901
Fred Harvey/Volz Collection

Hololokatsina (right center)
Catalog number: 910CI
Height: 7.25 in.
Date: pre-1901
Fred Harvey/Volz Collection

Muuyawkatsina (right)
Catalog number: 786CI
Height: 8.5 in.
Date: pre-1901
Fred Harvey/Volz Collection

p. 49
Kokopölö (left)
Catalog number: 898CI
Height: 14.25 in.
Date: pre-1900
Fred Harvey/Volz Collection

Kokopölö (right)
Catalog number: 899CI
Height: 9.75 in.
Date: pre-1900
Fred Harvey/Volz Collection

p. 50
Ma'lo
Catalog number: 811CI
Height: 11.25 in.
Date: pre-1901
Fred Harvey/Volz Collection

p. 51
Ma'lo
Catalog number: 916CI
Height: 11 in.
Date: pre-1901
Fred Harvey/Volz Collection

p. 51
Paalölöqangkatsina
Catalog number: NA-SW-HO-F-22
Height: 8 in.
Date: 1900–1920s
Original Heard Collection

p. 52
Manang'yakatsina
Catalog number: NA-SW-HO-F-132
Height: 10 in.
Date: 1940s–1950s
Goldwater Collection

p. 53
Tangaktsina
Catalog number: 776CI
Height: 14 in.
Date: pre-1901
Fred Harvey/Volz Collection

p. 53
Hanomana (left)
Catalog number: 924CI
Height: 7.5 in.
Date: pre-1901
Fred Harvey/Volz Collection

Mongwu (left center)
Catalog number: NA-SW-HO-F-716
Carver: Manfred Susunkewa
Height: 10.38 in.
Date: 1984
Museum Purchase

Hahay'iwuuti (right center)
Catalog number: 612CI
Height: 6.25 in.
Date: 1911–1913
Fred Harvey/Owen Collection

Salakmana (right)
Catalog number: 819CI
Height: 12 in.
Date: c. 1900
Fred Harvey/Volz Collection

p. 54
Morivoskatsina (left)
Catalog number: NA-SW-HO-F-397
Height: 9 in.
Date: 1900–1920
Goldwater Collection

Ngayayataqa (left center)
Catalog number: NA-SW-HO-F-182
Carver: Oswald White Bear Fredericks
Height: 11 in.
Date: 1959
Goldwater Collection

Morivoskatsina (right center)
Catalog number: NA-SW-HO-F-363
Height: 8 in.
Date: c. 1900
Goldwater Collection

Ngayayataqa (right)
Catalog number: NA-SW-HO-F-121
Carver: Oswald White Bear Fredericks
Height: 12 in.
Date: 1959
Goldwater Collection

p. 55
Hoolikatsina (left)
Catalog number: 1190CI
Height: 9 in.
Date: pre-1903
Fred Harvey/Voth Collection

Hoolikatsina (right)
Catalog number: NA-SW-HO-F-329
Height: 11 in.
Date: 1930s
Goldwater Collection

p. 56
Qömuvho'te (left)
Catalog number: 1177CI
Height: 9.5 in.
Date: pre-1903
Fred Harvey/Voth Collection

Sakwaho'te (left center)
Catalog number: NA-SW-HO-F-119
Carver: Oswald White Bear Fredericks
Height: 12 in.
Date: c. 1960
Goldwater Collection

Qömuvho'te (right center)
Catalog number: NA-SW-HO-F-108
Height: 9.5 in.
Date: 1930s
Goldwater Collection

Si'oho'te (right)
Catalog number: 858CI
Height: 10.5 in.
Date: pre-1901
Fred Harvey/Volz Collection

p. 57
Hehey'akatsina (left)
Catalog number: NA-SW-HO-F-245
Height: 8 in.
Date: 1900–1930
Goldwater Collection

Hehey'akatsina (left center)
Catalog number: NA-SW-HO-F-107
Carver: Oswald White Bear Fredericks
Height: 12 in.
Date: 1960
Goldwater Collection

Hehey'akatsina (right center)
Catalog number: NA-SW-HO-F-350
Height: 14 in.
Date: 1920s–1930s
Goldwater Collection

Hehey'akatsina (right)
Catalog number: NA-SW-HO-F-300
Height: 6 in.
Date: 1900
Goldwater Collection

p. 58
Hospowi (left)
Catalog number: NA-SW-HO-F-616
Carver: Se-Ona
Height: 13.5 in.
Date: 1975
Gift of Byron Hunter, Jr.

Pawikya (left center)
Catalog number: 792CI
Height: 12.25 in.
Date: pre-1901
Fred Harvey/Volz Collection

Tootsa (right center)
Catalog number: NA-SW-HO-F-200
Height: 11 in.
Date: 1920s–1930s
Goldwater Collection

Tootsa (right)
Catalog number: NA-SW-HO-F-529
Height: 9 in.
Date: c. 1970
Byron Harvey, III, Collection

p. 59
Payik'ala (left photo)
Catalog number: NA-SW-HO-F-74
Height: 12 in.
Date: 1900–1930
Goldwater Collection

p. 59
Payik'ala (right photo)
Catalog number: NA-SW-HO-F-708
Height: 13.75 in.
Date: 1970s
Museum Purchase

p. 60
Korososta
Catalog number: 1196CI
Height: 12 in.
Date: pre-1903
Fred Harvey/Voth Collection

p. 61
Hootsani
Catalog number: 865CI
Height: 14.5 in.
Date: pre-1901
Fred Harvey/Volz Collection

p. 61
Hewtomana
Catalog number: NA-SW-HO-F-477
Height: 13.5 in.
Date: c. 1960
Goldwater Collection

p. 62
Tsa'kwynakatsina (left)
Catalog number: 1159CI
Height: 10.5 in.
Date: pre-1903
Fred Harvey/Voth Collection

Tsa'kwaynakatsina (right)
Catalog number: 775CI
Height: 12.75 in.
Date: pre-1901
Fred Harvey/Volz Collection

p. 63
Nuvaktsina
Catalog number: NA-SW-HO-F-23
Height: 11 in.
Date: 1910–1945
Original Heard Collection

p. 65
Patsootskatsina (left)
Catalog number: NA-SW-HO-F-115
Carver: Oswald White Bear Fredericks
Height: 12 in.
Date: 1960
Goldwater Collection

Nana'tsuvsikyavo (center)
Catalog number: NA-SW-HO-F-232
Carver: Oswald White Bear Fredericks
Height: 12 in.
Date: c. 1960
Goldwater Collection

Navantsitsiklawqa (right)
Catalog number: NA-SW-HO-F-113
Carver: Oswald White Bear Fredericks
Height: 12 in.
Date: 1960
Goldwater Collection

p. 66
Koyemsi (left)
Catalog number: NA-SW-HO-F-742
Carver: Henry Shelton
Height: 8.75 in.
Date: c. 1980
Gift of Mr. and Mrs. Thomas White

Letotovi (left center)
Catalog number: NA-SW-HO-F-170
Carver: Oswald White Bear Fredericks
Height: 10 in.
Date: 1959
Goldwater Collection

Kokopölmana (right center)
Catalog number: 1197CI
Height: 9.25 in.
Date: pre-1903
Fred Harvey/Voth Collection

Koona (right)
Catalog number: NA-SW-HO-F-16
Height: 8.5 in.
Date: c. 1920
Original Heard Collection

p. 66
Koyemsi
Catalog number: NA-SW-HO-F-756
Carver: Brian Honyouti
Height: 9.75 in.
Date: 1975
Museum Purchase

p. 67
Sivutotovi
Catalog number: NA-SW-H0-F-406
Height: 11 in.
Date: 1900–1920
Goldwater Collection

Kokopölmana
Catalog number: 916CI
Height: 7.67 in.
Date: pre-1901
Fred Harvey/Volz Collection

Aykatsina
Catalog number: 793CI
Height: 13.26 in.
Date: pre-1901
Fred Harvey/Volz Collection

Kokopölmana
Catalog number: NA-SW-HO-F-304
Height: 7 in.
Date: 1930s-1940s
Goldwater Collection

Sivukwewtaqa
Catalog number: 851CI
13.6 in.
Date: pre-1901
Fred Harvey/Volz Collection

p.68
Malatsvetaqa (left)
Catalog number: NA-SW-HO-F-485
Carver: Vincent Selina
Height: 11.5 in.
Date: 1969
Byron Harvey, III, Collection

Sösö'pa (left center)
Catalog number: NA-SW-HO-F-344
Carver: Oswald White Bear Fredericks
Height: 11 in.
Date: 1959
Goldwater Collection

Sösö'pa (center)
Catalog number: NA-SW-HO-F-528
Carver: Clyde Honyouti
Height: 8.5 in.
Date: c. 1970
Byron Harvey, III, Collection

Hömsona (right center)
Catalog number: NA-SW-HO-F-174
Carver: Oswald White Bear Fredericks
Height: 11 in.
Date: 1959
Goldwater Collection

Kiisa (right)
Catalog number: NA-SW-HO-F-448
Height: 10 in.
Date: c. 1968
Museum Purchase

p. 69
Malatsvetaqa
Catalog number: NA-SW-HO-F-92
Carver: Oswald White Bear Fredericks
Height: 12 in.
Date: 1960
Goldwater Collection

p. 70
Poos'humkatsina
Catalog number: 873CI
Height: 11 in.
Date: pre-1901
Fred Harvey/Volz Collection

p. 71
Poos'humkatsina
Catalog number: NA-SW-HO-F-388
Height: 9 in.
Date: 1900–1920
Goldwater Collection

p. 72
Qa'ökatsina
Catalog number: NA-SW-HO-F-574
Carver: Calvin Dallas
Height: 14.25 in.
Date: 1974
Museum Purchase

p. 72
Avatshoya
Catalog number: NA-SW-HO-F-172
Carver: Oswald White Bear Fredericks
Height: 12 in.
Date: c. 1960
Goldwater Collection

p. 73
Sootantaqa
Catalog number: NA-SW-HO-F-714
Height: 13 in.
Date: 1983
Museum Purchase

p. 74
Hopi'avatshoya
Catalog number: NA-SW-HO-F-62
Carver: Oswald White Bear Fredericks
Height: 12 in.
Date: 1959
Goldwater Collection

p. 74
Koyemsi (left)
Catalog number: NA-SW-HO-F-648
Carver: Peter Shelton
Height: 11.75 in.
Date: c. 1978
Gift of Mr. Michael Mulberger

Koyemsi (right)
Catalog number: 785CI
Height: 7.75 in.
Date: pre-1901
Fred Harvey/Volz Collection

p. 75
Marawkatsina (left)
Catalog number: 770CI
Height: 16 in.
Date: pre-1901
Fred Harvey/Volz Collection

Marawkatsina (right)
Catalog number: 773CI
Height: 16.25 in.
Date: pre-1901
Fred Harvey/Volz Collection

p. 76
Navankatsina (left)
Catalog number: NA-SW-HO-F-103
Height: 11 in.
Date: 1940–1950
Goldwater Collection

Navankatsina (right)
Catalog number: NA-SW-HO-F-632
Height: 14 in.
Date: 1920s–1940s
Heard Museum Collection

p. 76
Puutskohu
Catalog number: NA-SW-HO-F-351
Height: 11 in.
Date: 1920–1930
Goldwater Collection

p. 77
Qa'ökatsina/Ngayayataqa
Catalog number: NA-SW-HO-F-161
Height: 11 in.
Date: c. 1910
Goldwater Collection

p. 78
Omawkatsina
Catalog number: 767CI
Height: 15.75 in.
Date: pre-1901
Fred Harvey/Volz Collection

p. 79
Angaktsina (left)
Catalog number: 883CI
Height: 10.5 in.
Date: pre-1901
Fred Harvey/Volz Collection

Angaktsina (left center)
Catalog number: NA-SW-HO-F-43
Height: 12 in.
Date: 1950–1960
Goldwater Collection

Angaktsina (center)
Catalog number: 837CI
Height: 10 in.
Date: pre-1901
Fred Harvey/Volz Collection

Angaktsina (right center)
Catalog number: NA-SW-HO-F-44
Height: 13.5 in.
Date: 1950–1960
Goldwater Collection

Takurmana (right)
Catalog number: 791CI
Height: 8.5 in.
Date: pre-1901
Fred Harvey/Volz Collection

p. 79
Koo'aakatsina (left)
Catalog number: 876CI
Height: 12 in.
Date: pre-1901
Fred Harvey/Volz Collection

Koo'aakatsina (center)
Catalog number: 878CI
Height: 13 in.
Date: pre-1901
Fred Harvey/Volz Collection

Koo'aakatsina (right)
Catalog number: NA-SW-HO-F-339
Height: 12 in.
Date: 1900–1920
Goldwater Collection

p. 80
Koo'aakatsina
Catalog number: NA-SW-HO-F-543
Height: 11.5 in.
Date: 1950s–1960s
Byron Harvey, III, Collection

p. 81
Tasavkatsina (left)
Catalog number: NA-SW-HO-F-204
Height: 12 in.
Date: 1940s–1950s
Goldwater Collection

Tasavkatsina (left center)
Catalog number: NA-SW-HO-F-326
Height: 11 in.
Date: 1930s
Goldwater Collection

Tasavkatsina (right center)
Catalog number: 859CI
Height: 13 in.
Date: early 1900s
Fred Harvey Collection

Tasavkatsina (right)
Catalog number: NA-SW-HO-F-97
Height: 12 in.
Date: 1940s–1950s
Goldwater Collection

p. 82
Yé'ii Bicheii (left)
Catalog number: NA-SW-NA-I-5
Carver: Navajo made
Height: 13.5 in.
Date: 1910
Heard Museum Collection

Yé'ii Bicheii (right)
Catalog number: NA-SW-HO-F-713
Height: 8.5 in.
Date: 1970s
Museum Purchase

p. 82
Tasavkatsina
Catalog number: NA-SW-HO-F-482
Height: 15.5 in.
Date: 1970
Byron Harvey, III, Collection

p. 83
Kwivikatsina (left)
Catalog number: NA-SW-HO-F-39
Height: 9.5 in.
Date: c. 1920s
Heard Museum Collection

Kwivikatsina (left center)
Catalog number: NA-SW-HO-F-712
Height: 13.25 in.
Date: c. 1980
Museum Purchase

Kwivikatsina (right center)
Catalog number: NA-SW-HO-F-430
Height: 13 in.
Date: 1955–1964
Goldwater Collection

Tonaylili (right)
Catalog number: (right) NA-SW-HO-F-580
Height: 10.25 in.
Date: c. 1970
Gift of Senator Barry M. Goldwater
    (not from original collection)

p. 83
Koninkatsina (left)
Catalog number: NA-SW-HO-F-106
Height: 10 in.
Date: 1900–1910
Goldwater Collection

Koninkatsina (center)
Catalog number: 787CI
Height: 11 in.
Date: pre-1901
Fred Harvey/Volz Collection

Koninkatsina (right)
Catalog number: 1237CI
Height: 12.75 in.
Date: pre-1903
Fred Harvey/Voth Collection

p. 84
Mongwu
Catalog number: NA-SW-HO-F-619
Carver: Alvin James, Sr.
Height: 17.5 in.
Date: 1974
Museum Purchase

p. 85
Tsuku (left)
Catalog number: NA-SW-HO-F-148
Height: 10 in.
Goldwater Collection

Koyaala (left center)
Catalog number: NA-SW-HO-F-257
Height: 6 in.
Date: 1900
Goldwater Collection

Tsuku (center)
Catalog number: NA-SW-HO-F-207
Height: 12 in.
Goldwater Collection

Koyaala (right center)
Catalog number: 931CI
Height: 7.5 in.
Date: pre-1901
Fred Harvey/Volz Collection

Koyaala (right)
Catalog number: NA-SW-HO-F-541
Height: 12 in.
Date: c. 1969
Byron Harvey, III, Collection

p. 87
Tseveyo
Catalog number: NA-SW-HO-F-205
Height: 12 in.
Date: 1920s–1940s
Goldwater Collection

p. 89
Katsinmana (left)
Catalog number: NA-SW-HO-F-282
Height: 8 in.
Date: 1900–1920s
Goldwater Collection

Hemiskatsina/Nimankatsina (center)
Catalog number: 762CI
Height: 14 in.
Date: pre-1901
Fred Harvey/Volz Collection

Katsinmana (right)
Catalog number: NA-SW-HO-F-8
Height: 8.5 in.
Date: 1930s
Original Heard Collection

p. 90
Qötsamana (left)
Catalog number: NA-SW-HO-F-79
Height: 7.5 in.
Goldwater Collection

Qötsamana (right)
Catalog number: 1222CI
Height: 9 in.
Date: pre-1903
Fred Harvey/Voth Collection

p. 90
Sio'hemiskatsina
Catalog number: (left) 761CI
Height: 18.5 in.
Date: pre-1901
Fred Harvey/Volz Collection

Hohomana (right)
Catalog number: 600CI
Height: 6.75 in.
Date: 1900–1920s
Fred Harvey Collection

p. 91
Sio'hemiskatsina (left)
Catalog number: 1157CI
Height: 16.75 in.
Date: pre-1903
Fred Harvey/Voth Collection

Nimankatsina (right)
Catalog number: 302CI
Height: 16.5 in.
Date: 1900
Fred Harvey Collection

p. 92
Ewtoto (left)
Catalog number: NA-SW-HO-F-589
Carver: Leo Lacapa, Jr.
Height: 12.25 in.
Date: 1970s
Gift of Senator Barry M. Goldwater
    (not from original collection)

Hemiskatsina (center)
Catalog number: 762CI
Height: 14 in.
Date: pre-1901
Fred Harvey/Volz Collection

Katsinmana (right)
Catalog number: 782CI
Height: 12.5 in.
Date: pre-1901
Fred Harvey/Volz Collection

p. 92
Maasawkatsina
Catalog number: NA-SW-HO-F-743
Carver: Wilbert Talashoma
Height: 11 in.
Date: c. 1980
Gift of Mr. and Mrs. Thomas White

p. 93
Maasawkatsina
Catalog number: NA-SW-HO-F-315
Height: 12 in.
Date: 1920s–1930s
Goldwater Collection

p. 93
Maasawkatsinmana
Catalog number: NA-SW-HO-F-744
Carver: Wilbert Talashoma
Height: 8.75 in.
Date: c. 1980
Gift of Mr. and Mrs. Thomas White

p. 94
Tawakatsina (left)
Catalog number: NA-SW-HO-F-490
Carver: Marshall Lomakema
Height: 18 in.
Date: c. 1970
Byron Harvey, III, Collection

Qa'ötorikiwtaqa (center)
Catalog number: NA-SW-HO-F-177
Height: 10 in.
Date: 1955
Goldwater Collection

Tawakatsina (right)
Catalog number: NA-SW-HO-F-578
Carver: Jimmie Kewanwytewa
Height: 10.5 in.
Date: c. 1950s
Goldwater Collection

p. 94
Hohotaqa
Catalog number: 1163CI
Height: 10.5 in.
Date: pre-1903
Fred Harvey/Voth Collection

p. 95
Owakkatsina (left)
Catalog number: 771CI
Height: 12 in.
Date: pre-1901
Fred Harvey/Volz Collection

Owakkatsina (right)
Catalog number: 772CI
Height: 12 in.
Date: pre-1901
Fred Harvey/Volz Collection

p. 95
Wukoqalakatsina (left)
Catalog number: 833CI
Height: 13 in.
Date: pre-1901
Fred Harvey/Volz Collection

Wukoqalakatsina (right)
Catalog number: 1149CI
Height: 11.5 in.
Date: pre-1903
Fred Harvey/Voth Collection

GLOSSARY

Aalosaka: The supreme being of the Two-Horn society

Ahöla: A katsina priest of a high order

Ahölatmana'at: A katsina maiden who accompanies the Ahöla

Áholi: An Orayvi (Third Mesa) winter solstice katsina appearing during Powamuya

Ahölwutaqa: An elderly, wise chief katsina

ala: A horn (see Payik'ala)

Angaktsina: A Longhair katsina rain god

Angk'wa: A series of katsina night dances

Angwusnasomtaqa: A katsina Mother with many roles and responsibilities

askwali: Hopi female usage meaning "thank you"

Avatshoya: A White Corn katsina representing excellent crop yield and bountiful harvest

Awhalayni: A Soyalkatsina who appears during winter solstice season

Aykatsina: A Rattle Racer katsina

Ewizro: A Warrior katsina who appears during Powamuya and the summer katsina day dances

Ewtoto: A katsina spiritual father

Haaniiya: An Ogre katsina appearing during Powamuya and Angk'wa

Hahay'iwuuti: An energetic, sprightful, talkative Mother of the katsinam; also a maiden who accompanies the Hemiskatsinam at Niman ceremony

haki: To wait

Hakitonmuya: A period sometime in May; to delay planting until warm weather in June

Hakit'uyis: The season for planting beans, pumpkin, gourd, watermelon, etc.

Hanomana: An unmarried katsina maiden of the Hano village of First Mesa

Hee'e'e: A Warrior katsina maiden who appears during Powamuya to lead the family of Whipper katsinam into the village

Hehey'akatsina: A handsome messenger katsina to the cloud gods who talks "backwards," or says the opposite of what he means

Hehey'amuytaaha'am: An Uncle whose words have opposite meaning;
 also a clown

Hemiskatsinam: See Nimankatsinam

Hewtokatsinam: Katsinam who bring cold moisture

Hewtom: A group of Hewtokatsinam

Hewtomana: Katsina maiden to Hewtom, Tsakwaynam or Tsitsinom

Hiilili: A Whipper katsina who is very spirited in action

Hohomana: The female Milky Way katsina who accompanies the
 Hemiskatsinam at the Niman ceremony

hohongvitu: The ritual energy source for human racers' strength and
 endurance

Hohotaqa: A male Milky Way katsina related to the Hohomana

Hololokatsinam: A katsina who assists in maintaining a balance in the
 universe

hömsomi: A traditional Hopi male hairstyle, such as a "bun"

Hömsona: A black-faced Racer katsina who snips a crop of hair from
 his opponents

Honankatsina: The Badger katsina

Honkatsina: The Bear katsina

Hoolikatsinam: Katsina messengers to the rain gods

Hootsani: An old katsina introduced to Hopi by the Pueblos of
 Rio Grande

Hopi'avatshoya: An original Hopi White Corn katsina

Hopituy: Specific to the Hopi

Hospowi: The Roadrunner katsina

Ho'te: A messenger katsina to the rain gods

Ho'tekatsinam: Several katsina rain god messengers

Ho'tem: A group of Ho'tekatsinam

Hototöm: Racer katsinam who appear to challenge the village men
 and boys to footraces

katsina: A benevolent spirit being

katsinam: Plural for katsina

katsinavitu: A pair of katsinam or two different kinds of katsinam

katsinmamantu: Plural for katsinmana

katsinmana: A katsina maiden

katsinmanavitu: A pair of katsina maidens or two different kinds of
 katsina maidens

Kawaykatsina: A Horse katsina, one of the many animal katsinam
 who appear during Angk'wa or the summer katsina day dances

kawayo: Watermelon or watermelons

Kelmuya: A season in November in which the Hopi religious calendar
 is formalized and decreed

Kiisa: A Chicken Hawk Racer katsina who carries a maawiki to whip his opponents with when he catches them

kikmongwi: A village chief

kiva: A ceremonial chamber or chambers

Kokopölmaman't: Plural for Kokopölmana

Kokopölmana: A female Racer fertility spirit being who intercepts the katsina Racers' opponents and makes copulatory gestures to promote the procreation of life

Kokopölmanavitu: A pair of female fertility spirit beings

Kokopölö: A humpback fertility spirit being appearing during Angk'wa

Kokosorhoya: A very young katsina who is innocent and pure of heart and represents all kinds of seeds

Kokosors: A spirit who causes seeds to sprout or develop to enhance crop growth

koletviki: Blue cornmeal bread baked on a hot piki-stone

Konin: Maidens who accompany the Koninkatsinam

Koninkatsinam: The Hopi version of katsinam that honor and depict the Havasupai tribe (not borrowed from the Havasupai: katsinam are unique to the Pueblo Indian tribes of Arizona and New Mexico)

Koo'aakatsina: An old Hopi katsina who represents rain and is a messenger to the rain gods

Koona: A Chipmunk Racer katsina who is very fast on his feet

Korososta: A katsina who brings various types of seeds for planting

Koyaala: Hano clown (of Hano Village on First Mesa)

Koyemsi: A Mudhead katsina who portrays different characters

Koyemsihoyam: Young Mudheads who convey their mischievousness by pulling on the ceremonial dress of the Wupamokatsina, who in turn whips them to correct their behavior.

Koyemsimu: Several Mudhead katsinam

kuy'wiki: A jug of water that has been spiritually blessed

kwaani: Dried figs given to the people by the Koninkatsinam

Kwahu: An Eagle katsina

kwakha: Hopi male usage meaning "thank you"

Kwarunakvuhooli: A katsina who has eagle tail feathers in place of ears

Kwewu: A Wolf katsina

Kwikwilyaqa: A Striped-Nose katsina who portrays different personalities by mocking people or other katsinam

Kwivikatsinam: Showy Navajo katsinam who are very handsome and dressy

kwiya: Windbreaks constructed in the fields to protect plant seedlings

Kwiyamuya: A season in early spring (around April) when the fields

are prepared for planting of early corn and construction of windbreaks (kwiya) to protect the seedlings

Kyaamuya: "Greatness of the season"; winter solstice season

kyamuy: Specific to paternal aunts

Kyaro: The Parrot katsina

Lakon: Second of three women's societies; the Basket Dance performed by women

Lakontataqtu: Male members initiated into the Lakon society

Lelentu: The Flute ceremony

Lenangkatsina: A Soyalkatsina appearing during winter solstice season

Lenangmana: A female member of the Lenangkatsinam

Lenangtaqa: A male Flute deity

Letotovi: A Mosquito Racer katsina who sharply whips his opponents:
the blows feel like mosquito bites

Maasawkatsina: An Earth God katsina who is believed to remain with
the Hopi the entire year

Maasawkatsinavitu: A pair of Earth God katsinam

Maasawkatsinmana: A female Earth God katsina

Maasawu: The Earth god; a supreme deity in the Fourth World

maawiki: A short magical wand used for blessing purposes by the
Maasawu or other spirit beings; also a stuffed whip used by the
Kiisa to whip his opponents with when he catches them

Malatsvetaqa: A Handprint Racer katsina who uses soot mixed with
grease to leave his handprint on his opponents

Ma'lo: The Cloud-Bringing katsina who wears a band of cloud
symbols around the forehead and performs a dance that portrays
a prayer for rain

Mamalotu: Plural for Ma'lo

mana: An unmarried female; a maiden

Manang'yakatsina: The Chameleon katsina; a messenger to the rain
gods

Maraw: Third of three women's societies

Marawkatsina: Stylish katsina who represents moisture, is a messenger to the rain gods, and whose headdress is like that of the
Marawmana

Marawwimi: First of three women's societies

Mastopkatsina: A member of the Soyal season katsinam (appearing
only on Third Mesa); a counterpart of Second Mesa's Sivuktsina

mata: Grinding stone for cornmeal

melooni: Muskmelon or muskmelons

Mongkatsinam: Chief katsinam having leadership duties and responsibilities

mongwi: A chief having leadership duties and responsibilities

Mongwu: A Great-Horned Owl katsina

mööyi: A paternal nephew or niece

morivosi: A vegetable; bean or beans

Morivoskatsina: A Bean katsina who brings a variety of beans for planting

Mosayurkatsinam: Several Buffalo katsinam

Motsinkatsina: The Disheveled Hair katsina having policing responsibilities at public work projects, making sure that all available men are assisting

Muuyawkatsina: The Moon katsina who assists in maintaining a balance in the universe

Muuyawu: The moon

Muyingwa: The Germination God katsina

Nana'tsuvsikyavo: A Hesitant Yellow-Eyed Racer katsina, a humble challenger

Nasanmuya: The harvest season or feast period (sometime in September)

Nata'aska: A Bigmouthed Ogre katsina: Uncle in the Ogre family who sings about eating children

nat'wani: Home-grown crops or vegetables

Navankatsina: A Velvet-Shirt katsina representing the blooming of plant life and focusing on the beauty of life

Navantsitsiklawqa: A Shirt-Ripper Racer katsina who tears his opponents' shirts when he catches them

Ngayayataqa: See Qa'ökatsina

ngoytiwya: A Hopi tradition in which men and boys carry home-grown produce and run around joyfully yelling "ya ha ha" while paternal aunts make an effort to take away the produce

ngumni: A finely ground cornmeal

Niman: "Going home"; after the Niman ceremony in July, the katsinam return to their spiritual homes

Nimankatsinam: Home Dance katsinam appearing during Niman ceremony, also called *Hemiskatsinam*

Nimankatsinmuy: Specific to Nimankatsinam

Nimanmuya: A season for the Niman ceremony (sometime in July)

Nimantiikive: The katsina Home Dance or Niman ceremony

noova: A variety of breads and pastry

nöqkwivi: A stew

Nuvaktsina: A Snow katsina

Omawkatsina: A Cumulus Cloud katsina representing rain clouds and summer cloud bursts giving growth to plant life

Ösömuya: The katsina night dance season (sometime in March)

ovaa: A white, woven wedding robe

Owaktsinam: Coal katsinam who represent the minerals and their beneficial values for the people

O'waqölt: The Basket Dance, performed by women

Paalölöqangkatsina: A Water Serpent katsina

Paamuya: Winter social dances (sometime in January)

paatnga: Various types of pumpkin

paayom: Numeral three

Palhikmamant: Plural for Palhikmana

Palhikmamantu: Another plural for Palhikmana

Palhikmana: A katsina maiden with several functions; she can appear during Angk'wa as a Poliimana, as a corn-grinding maiden, or perform a special dance

Pangkatsina: A Big-Horn Sheep katsina

Pangkatsinam: A group of Big-Horn Sheep katsinam

Pangwu: A Big-Horn sheep katsina

Patsootskatsina: A Cockleburr Racer katsina who rubs cockleburrs in his opponents' hair when he catches them

Pawikya: A Duck katsina whose feathers are used by the Hopi

Payik'ala: A Three-Horned katsina, messenger to the rain gods

pik'ami: A sweet corn pudding; a type of Hopi traditional bread

piki: A very thin, rolled sheet of blue cornmeal

Pivtukam: Several katsina clowns

Poliimana: Butterfly Maiden katsina; a counterpart of the Palhikmana, appearing as the Corn Grinding Maiden during night dances

Poliitaqa: A male Butterfly katsina; a dancing partner of the Poliimana

Pöma'uyis: The early planting season of different kinds of early corn (sometime in April)

poos'humi: Plant seeds of different types

Poos'humkatsina: A Seed katsina who brings different types of seeds for planting

Pootawikkatsina: A Coiled Plaque Carrier katsina who brings brightly decorated plaques as gifts for the people

Powamuya: A ceremonial season (sometime in February), depicting the final stages of world creation and imploring the katsina spirits to carry out the purification of life

Powamuykatsinam: Katsinam who dance at Powamuya

Powamuymaman't: Several katsina maidens who accompany their male counterparts in carrying out the Powamuy dance

Puutskohu: A Rabbit Stick katsina, who symbolically brings the art of hunting for men and represents the increase in game animals for life nourishment

Qaletaqa: A Warrior katsina who protects the Soyal rituals, ensuring that they are carried out uninterrupted

Qa'ökatsina: A Corn katsina representing different types of sacred corn, also called Ngayayataqa

Qa'ötorikiwtaqa: A Corn katsina who wears two strings of different colors of corn, over the shoulders, crisscrossed in front and back of body

qa'öwiki: A string of corn of assorted colors

Qömuvho'tem: Katsina messengers to the rain gods, whose heads are black with different color decorations

Qöqlo: A katsina who appears at the Powamuya, representing different characters, such as artists, creating and bringing colorful gifts, and storytellers, telling a story symbolic of pleasantness for all mankind

Qöqöqlom: Katsinam who bring bean sprouts and colorful gifts for their friends, the village people

Qötsamanavitu: A pair of Snow katsina maidens who accompany the Hemiskatsinam during the Niman ceremony

Qötsawihazru: A White Ogre katsina; Uncle of the Ogre family who is not active but still fearsome

sakwa: The color blue

Sakwaho'te: Uncle of the mixed katsinam whose head and body is painted the color blue and who dances to the side guarding the katsinam

Salakmana: A katsina maiden whose tall and slender body stands about eight feet

Salako: A katsina who stands about eight feet tall and could be male or female

sikwi: Meat of wild game

Sikyaqöqlo: A katsina who is an artist who practices the art of the agrarian culture, and is a storyteller

Sikyatsungtaqa: A Third Mesa Hooli katsina whose lips are yellow in color, known on Second Mesa as Susuk'holi

sinom: The Hopi people (as used here)

Si'ohemiskatsina: Zuni Home Dancer

Si'oho'te: A katsina spirit from the Zuni Pueblo

Sipiknikatsina: A Whipper katsina who is a guard

Sipiknitaqa: A Whipper katsina of the masculine gender

Sivuktsina: A katsina representing the energy of fertility for mankind

Sivuktsinam: Katsina spirits who promote the procreation of life

Sivuktsinavitu: A pair of Sivuktsinam

Sivukwewtaqa: A katsina who wears black body paint around the waist

Sivutotovi: A Blackfly Racer katsina who carries a short yucca whip for whipping his opponents: the blows feel like fly stings

Sola'wutsi: The Zuni Fire God, a very young katsina who carries a torch

somiviki: Corn pudding wrapped in corn husk

so'oh: A paternal grandmother

Soo'so'yokt: The Ogre family

Soo'so'yoktu: Another name for the Ogre family

sootanta: A dance motion with the appearance of poking or prodding

Sootantaqa: A Corn Dancer katsina, whose dance motion has the appearance of poking or prodding

Sootukwnang: A Star katsina, a spirit deity who maintains the balance of the universe

sooya: A planting stick

Sösö'pa: A Cricket Racer katsina who whips his opponents gently with a yucca shoot

Soyal: The winter solstice ceremony

Soyalangwu: A period of the Soyal ceremony, a time for reverence and respect for the spirits

Soyalkatsina: A katsina who comes during winter solstice season

Soyalmuya: Winter solstice season

Soyalwimi: A sacred ceremony blessing the renewal of life, held in December

So'yok'ki: The spiritual home of the Ogres

So'yoktaqa: The husband of the So'yokwuuti

So'yokwuuti: A sister of the Ogre family

Susuk'holi: The Hooli katsina whose name is derived from wearing only four eagle tail feathers, "singly" worn hanging on each side of the ears; known as Sikyatsungtaqa on Third Mesa

suta: Red sienna

Takurmana: A Yellow Corn katsina maiden who represents rain

takurqa'ö: Yellow corn

Talangva: The summer season (around July)

Tala'paamuya: The summer social dance season (sometime in August)

Tangaktsina: A Rainbow katsina, representing moisture of rain, and a rain god messenger

Tasavkatsinam: The Hopi version of katsinam that honor and depict the Navajo tribe (not *borrowed* from the Navajo: katsinam are unique to the Pueblo Indian tribes of Arizona and New Mexico)

tataqtu: Male dancing partners

Tawakatsina: The Sun katsina

tawaktsi: Sweet corn

tawiya: A gourd or gourds

tihu: Katsina doll

tiikive: A dance that may be one or two days

tiimayna: A formal presentation of the bride to the spirit beings; to present the bride

Toho'osmuya: The early stages of the winter solstice season (sometime in October)

Tokotsi: A Wildcat katsina; proneness to anger

Tokotskatsina: The Wildcat katsina

Tonaylili: An Uncle katsina; small river

toosi: Finely ground sweet cornmeal

Tootsa: A Hummingbird katsina

Tossonkoyemsi: The Mudhead katsina who appears with the Ogre family and who is the taster of toosi to determine its kind and quality

totokya: A period of days surrounding a dance or the dance day

Tsa'kwayna: A Warrior Uncle katsina spirit who came to Hopi from the Zuni Pueblo

Tsa'kwaynam: Several Warrior katsinam

Tsanayo: A Mongkatsina who appears during Powamuya

Tseveyo: An Ogre katsina who is a disciplinarian

Tsitoto: A Flower katsina

Tsitsinom: A Warrior katsinam who came to Hopi from the Pueblos of the Rio Grande

Tsivkatsina: An Antelope katsina

Tsuku: A Clown katsina, each village having its own version of dress and speech

tungni: A Hopi surname given to the eaglets

Tungwivkatsinam: Mongkatsinam who perform the initiation blessings into the katsina beliefs

tutskwa: The land

tuuwanasavi: The spiritual center of the earth, which was established and developed during the Hopi clan migrations

Tuuwaqatsi: The earth; Mother Earth

Tuvatsqöqlo: Black Qöqlo whose spoken words have the opposite meaning *uuaya'ta:* An organized planting party

Wakaskatsina: A Cow katsina and friendly spirit messenger to the rain
 gods

Wakaskatsinam: A group of Cow katsinam

Wiharu: An Ogre Uncle who desires fatty and greasy foods, or
 children who are obese, having flesh that is rich and tasty

wiqktö: Violet corn

Wukoqalakatsina: A Big-Forehead katsina believed to be borrowed
 from the Zuni Pueblo

Wuko'uyis: The main planting season in early June

Wupamokatsina: The Long Mouth katsina who is very dignified and
 supervises the security forces of the Whipper katsinam

wuuti: A married female

Wuutsimwimi: A sacred ceremony of one of the sacred religious orders
 for men

Yé'ii Bicheii: Navajo katsina Grandfather appearing with the
 Tasavkatsinam, dancing on the side, making arm and hand
 motions depicting the meaning of the song; a Hopi katsina depicting an elderly Navajo spirit being

FURTHER READING

MAGAZINES

Colton, Harold S. "What is a Kachina?" *Plateau* 19(1947): 40–47.

Hait, Pam. "The Hopi Tricentennial: The Great Pueblo Revolt Revisited." *Arizona Highways* 56, no. 9 (1980): 2–6.

Negri, Sam. "Kachina Carving: Artistry in Wood." *Arizona Highways* 69, no. 5 (1993): 14–17.

Page, Jake. "Inside the Sacred Hopi Homeland." *National Geographic* 162, no. 5 (1982): 607–629.

Wright, Barton. "The Search for Kokopelli." *Arizona Highways* 69, no. 7 (1993): 14–17.

BOOKS

Boissiere, Robert. *Meditations with the Hopi.* Santa Fe: Bear & Co., 1986.

Colton, Harold S. *Hopi Kachina Dolls: With a Key to Their Identification.* Albuquerque: University of New Mexico Press, 1949.

Dockstader, Frederick J. *The Kachina and the White Man: A Study of the Influences of White Culture on the Hopi Kachina Cult.* Albuquerque: University of New Mexico Press, 1985.

Fewkes, Jesse Walter. *Hopi Kachinas, Drawn by Native Artists.* Chicago: Rio Grande Press, 1962.

Hunt, W. Ben. *Kachina Dolls.* Milwaukee Public Museum, 1958.

James, Harry C. *Pages from Hopi History.* Tucson: University of Arizona Press, 1974.

Mora, Joseph. *The Year of the Hopi: Paintings and Photographs by Joseph Mora, 1904–06.* New York: Rizzoli, 1979.

Page, Jake and Susanne. *Hopi.* New York: Abrams, 1982.

Seaman, P. David. *Hopi Dictionary: Hopi-English, English-Hopi Grammatical Appendix.* Flagstaff, Department of Anthropology, Northern Arizona University, 1985.

Teiwes, Helga. *Kachina Dolls: The Art of Hopi Carvers.* Tucson: University of Arizona Press, 1991.

Washburn, Dorothy K., ed. *Hopi Kachina: Spirit of Life.* San Francisco: California Academy of Sciences, 1980.

Waters, Frank. *Book of the Hopi.* New York: Viking, 1963.

Wright, Barton. *Hopi Kachinas: The Complete Guide to Collecting Kachina Dolls.* Flagstaff: Northland Publishing, 1977.

———. *Kachinas: A Hopi Artist's Documentary.* Flagstaff: Northland Publishing with The Heard Museum, 1973.

———. *Kachinas: The Barry Goldwater Collection at The Heard Museum.* Phoenix: W.A. Krueger Co. with The Heard Museum, 1975.

INDEX

ABOUT THE AUTHOR

Elizabeth Alexander

Alph H. Secakuku was born in the Hopi village of Supawlavi on Second Mesa, Arizona, to the Snake Clan. His mother is a descendant of the Snake Clan people from the village of Paaqavi on Third Mesa.

Alph spent the first twenty years of his life on the Hopi Reservation, living and learning the traditions and cultural teachings of the Hopi. He voluntarily served in the U.S. Navy from 1960 to 1964, graduated from Northern Arizona University with a Bachelor of Science degree in Business Administration in 1968, and worked for the Bureau of Indian Affairs for twenty-four years, retiring in 1994.

Alph is self-employed as an artist (carver of katsina dolls, stone sculptor, and painter) and lecturer on the subject of Hopi tradition and culture. His wife, Alfreda, is a Hopi of the Paaqavi Clan, village of Paaqavi, Third Mesa. Their three children are Scott, Charles, and Tara.